Your Guide to Climate Action

How to move beyond your footprint and make a BIG impact

RYAN HAGEN

Copyright © 2025 Ryan Hagen. All rights reserved.

This is where I'm supposed to tell you to *not* reuse parts of this book.

But let's be real – the whole point of this book is to help people like you accelerate climate action. So, assuming you're like 99.9% of people and not a scammer, please quote from it for climate education and action (e.g., in a classroom, presentation, or blog post) – just give credit. If you want to reuse or share entire sections or chapters, just ask – I can give you a copy.

Teachers and nonprofits: If you want to make a bulk order, let me know and we can work out a discount.

And please let me know how it helps you – hearing from people always makes my day!

ryanhagen021@gmail.com

Edited by Larry Yu | Designed by Elizabeth Edwards

Published by Climate Action Press | First Edition

Written in Burlington, VT – the unceded territory of the Western Abenaki, whose history, wisdom, and stewardship are vital for healing our connection to nature and each other.

Library of Congress Control Number: 2025921086

ISBN: 979-8-9918256-1-0 (paperback)
ISBN: 979-8-9918256-2-7 (hardcover)
ISBN: 979-8-9918256-0-3 (e-book)

Contents

Preface	1
Introduction	5

Part 1: Understanding the Situation

1. The Big Picture	16
2. Getting Grounded: Navigating Eco-Emotions	27
3. What the World Needs To Do	35
4. What We Have Going For Us	47
5. Imagining a Better World	50

Part 2: Your Power to Change Systems

6. Small Groups of People Can Change Big Systems	60
7. You Are FAR More Powerful Than You Think	66

Part 3: What You Can Do: Top 10 Effective Actions

8. Finding Your Place in the Climate Movement	74
9. Talk About It!	81
10. Help Elect Climate Champions	93
11. Help Make Your Town or City Climate Positive	101
12. Help Make Your Company Climate Positive	112
13. Get a Climate Job	126
14. Help Make Your School Climate Positive	132
15. Minimize Your Carbon Footprint	141
16. Make Your Money Climate Positive	151
17. Donate to Nonprofits Doing Impactful Work	158
18. Peacefully Protesting & Civil Resistance	167

Part 4: On Moving Forward Wisely

19. Taking Care of Ourselves & Each Other	179
20. Shifting the Paradigm	183
21. What Matters Most?	189
Acknowledgments	196
Resources & Citations	200
About the Author	222

Preface

I want to start by sharing the 200 words I've spent more time on than any others in my life: my "Truths and Life Intentions." It's the only thing in this book that I didn't write for you. I wrote it in 2017 as a way to clarify what matters most to me.

I'm not sharing this deeply personal north star with any naive expectation that you'll adopt it. I'm sharing it because this book wouldn't exist without it. And because it'll give you a better understanding of me and where I'm coming from: how I think, what I care about, and who I'm striving to be.

One last thing to know: I'm still not very *good* at following all these intentions and keeping these truths in mind day-to-day. But I'm getting better over time. And that's the point.

Truths and Life Intentions

I am going to die. It could happen at any moment.

But I am here now, and that is truly a miracle.

All known life is a miracle. We live on Earth – just a pebble in the vast cosmos, our only home.

All life on Earth is biologically related – a family.

We are made of stardust. We are one.

I am aware my life simply consists of a multitude of nows. And do my best to live in the now as often as possible. It's all I'll ever have.

I will make the most of my time, being true to myself and living out my values.

I invest my precious time:
- *Loving myself.*
- *Loving family and friends.*
- *Loving all other life I interact with.*
- *Working to prolong the existence and maximize the quality of life on Earth.*

I do this because I love life. And I want as many people as possible to experience as good a life as possible, including people who aren't born yet like my kids and grandkids.

In my heart, I know contributing to others' happiness and making the world a better place is the right thing to do.

By being conscious of these truths and consistently acting on my intentions, I will flourish.

Writing this climate action guide was a way of loving all the people I know and the many beings I don't – a way to help "prolong the existence and maximize the quality of life on Earth." Because I'm convinced of two things:

1. The effects of climate and ecological breakdown will be **much worse** than most people expect.
2. We can rebuild a better society **much faster** than most anyone thinks is possible if enough people like you and me step up.

We tend to think linearly. But these environmental and social systems move exponentially. As Director of the Multisolving Institute, Dr. Elizabeth Sawin says, "When our problems grow exponentially, the danger is that we react too late. When our solutions grow exponentially, the danger is we give up too early."

I believe most people are good and want to do more to protect the people and places we love – to help build a better world. If that's you, you've found the right book. And I'm grateful we're on this journey together.

Much love,
Ryan

Introduction

Do you remember when the reality of climate change truly sank in for you?

For some, it happens in an instant – a sudden realization or an extreme lived experience like a wildfire, heatwave, or flood taking away a home, crops, or someone they love. For some, it's more gradual – a slow drip of conversations, headlines, and connecting dots that builds up over time. For some younger people, it's all they've ever known – an underlying anxiety about a crisis they didn't create but must face.

Everyone's path is different. But, eventually, we all end up at the same place. We realize we need to figure out *what the hell to do about it*.

You're here because you:

1. Know that climate and ecological breakdown threaten everything we care about,
2. Are rightfully worried (or freaking out),
3. Realize that the people in charge aren't doing anywhere near enough, and
4. Want to **do something** about it. You want to do **more** to help transform society toward a safer, healthier, and more just future where all life thrives.

I'm here for the exact same reasons. And we are not alone. Study after study shows there are billions of people around the world who feel the same way – who are worried about climate and want to do more to help.

This is welcome news because we're living through what may be the most disruptive and consequential chapter in human history. With each day that passes, human-caused global heating and ecosystem destruction make it harder to live. To stop making these problems worse, we must achieve net-zero emissions globally *and* become a planet-positive species that does more good than harm by restoring our life-supporting ecosystems.

What the planetary emergency means for life on Earth in the decades to come is daunting, scary, heartbreaking, infuriating, overwhelming, exhausting, and everything in between.

It's natural to feel these things. And, given the scale of the problem, it's rational to wonder: Is it too late? Does what I do make any difference?

These are important questions. So here are the quick answers:

It both is and isn't too late. It's too late because, after decades of delayed action, the climate has already changed. The climate and ecological crises are increasingly wreaking havoc by taking lives, destroying infrastructure, and unraveling the ecosystems that function as our life-support systems. And all of this will get worse before it gets better.

So the hard truth is that for far too many innocent people, places, wildlife, and ecosystems, action was or will be too late. This failure (and, in many ways, crime against humanity) is a historic, inexpressible injustice.

But at the same time, *it is not too late.*

The most important thing to understand about the future, as planetary futurist Alex Steffen often says, is this: There is still a *vast* difference between the best and worst-case scenarios. And the future we get depends on what each of us decides to do in the coming days, months, and years.

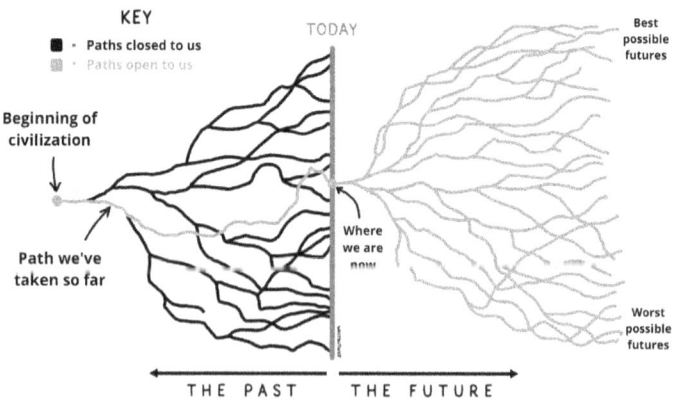

Pathways to best and worst possible futures.
Credit: Tim Urban, Wait But Why. (Labels modified)

There's still so much that hangs in the balance – so many lives we can help to save or improve, including our own and the people we love… or will love when they're born.

I'm writing this book because I know that no matter who you are, what you do, or where you live, you can help move us closer to the best-case future scenarios because **you are far more powerful than you realize**.

Every one of us influences the people around us, the community and state we live in, the schools we go to, and the organizations we work for.

Collectively, the policy and investment decisions made in these very same communities, states, schools, and organizations are what will determine our future.

So, as one of the relatively few people who belong to these places and know the people there, you are one of the relatively few people who can influence the crucial decisions being made there. It's the sum of all these decisions in our schools, communities, states, and companies that will determine how sustainable our world is going forward.

That means that **what you do matters**. What you choose to do (or not do) *does* make a difference.

Every one of us has something valuable to contribute. We all have different skills, experiences, resources, ideas, connections, and spheres of influence that we can gear toward solving this problem.

This book will help you understand your power and how to use it to change the systems you're a part of. It will also help you navigate your climate journey – a journey we'll all be on for the rest of our lives.

Great! And who are you exactly?

Right, hi :)

My name is Ryan Hagen, and I have been a full-on sustainability nerd since 2013.

The first time climate change crossed my radar, though, was in the spring of 2012 when I was 20 years old. My girlfriend at the time emailed me a link to a scientific study about it. I remember being slightly alarmed but quickly putting it out of my mind and moving on. It seemed overwhelming, sad, and scary. But I ultimately rationalized it away like most of us do with some combination of, "This sounds… pretty bad. But it also seems like it's a future problem? And maybe it's not as bad as it sounds. Nobody I know is talking about it. Neither is the media so it can't be *that* big of a deal, right? There's no use in worrying myself…plus I don't have time right now – I've got things to do and people to see."

Six months later, I watched *An Inconvenient Truth* while studying abroad in Copenhagen and was alarmed. I started researching. I got more freaked out. "This is real. And a big deal. Why isn't *everyone* talking about this? Why aren't we doing something about it?"

One day, I stumbled across a poll asking people to rank their political issues. At the time, I was trying to figure out what to do career-wise. I was in the middle of a summer internship at an insurance company that I now know is fueling the climate crisis. Week by week, I became increasingly convinced that if I was going to work 40 hours a week for the next 40 years, I needed to find work that was more meaningful. So I put a lot of thought into the question this poll was asking. What *was* the most important issue to me? The list of options read: Healthcare, The Economy, Taxes, Immigration, The Environment, National Security, etc. When I came to "The Environment" and compared it to the other issues one by one, I slowly realized it had to be the most important.

My logic was simple: We depend on the environment for our most basic needs, such as food, water, air, and safe places to live. If the environment was too polluted – if the weather and climate became too extreme – if the basic building blocks that every human relies on became too scarce, then none of the other things would matter all that much (if they still existed at all).

That was the moment I realized: If we get climate wrong, nothing else will be right. There would be unimaginable amounts of suffering, upheaval, and death. So many lives were at stake. And, on the flipside, *so many lives could be saved and improved if we took action to solve it.*

In the following months, it became clear that I couldn't unsee that truth. I knew I wouldn't be able to look at myself in the mirror if I ignored it – if I didn't at least *try* to do something about it. So I made a promise to myself that I'd find a way to make a career out of working on climate change.

After graduating from college with a business degree in economics and sustainability, I got a job working in clean technology. But a few years later, I was ready for a change. I quit to go backpacking and figure out how I could do more on climate. Increasing my positive impact felt even more urgent after Donald Trump got elected in 2016.

Days after leaving my job, a friend asked me if I'd write an article on sustainability for his blog. I was pretty stoked about the idea. I had A LOT to say – way too much for one article. In the following weeks, this seed of an idea grew from writing a single article to starting a newsletter that would empower people everywhere to act on climate. Once again, I knew I'd regret it if I didn't at least try. So, I listened to my heart and decided to start writing! …In other words, I moved back home with my parents to start Crowdsourcing Sustainability and pretty much everyone I knew thought I was nuts.

Crowdsourcing Sustainability was built around a weekly newsletter called "What on EARTH?!" that I wrote to educate, inspire, and empower people to act on climate. After a couple of long years, it took off with 200,000+ people signing up from 150+ countries. And I turned Crowdsourcing Sustainability into a nonprofit.

From 2017 to 2023, I wrote over 225 newsletters, pouring my heart and soul into every one. During that time, I also spoke with hundreds of people in the Crowdsourcing Sustainability community about their climate journeys and actions, interviewed dozens of sustainability leaders about what we can do, did *a ton* of research, made a lot of friends in the climate space, spoke at dozens of events, and was featured by the UN, TEDx, and LinkedIn Top Voices in the Green Economy for my work.

As I learned more about the most impactful actions we can take, I'd write about why they mattered and how to do them. In doing so, I helped inspire and empower thousands of people to take more, and more systemic, climate actions. Some people:

- Switched careers (e.g., from working on Facebook to food waste).
- Overcame anxiety and became activists working to get their schools, towns, and states to implement climate solutions.
- Started working to change policies and investments at their company.
- Got their universities to start green revolving funds to invest in sustainable projects.
- Began organizing their churches and clubs to accelerate action.

It was this process of identifying, researching, and guiding people on taking a variety of different climate actions that led to the top ten list featured in Part 3 of this book!

Crucial to all of this was my own activism and self-education along the way. I never stopped learning, doing the work, growing, and meeting amazing people. I went to Citizens' Climate Lobby's bootcamp and lobbying day, The Climate Reality Project's training with Al Gore, Project Drawdown's first two conferences (camping in freezing temps for one), and multiple Sunrise Movement trainings.

I became an activist with the Sunrise Movement, Extinction Rebellion, and an ally to Fridays for Future. I risked arrest multiple times (and actually got arrested for peacefully protesting with Sunrise in the halls of Congress for a Green New Deal). I've been that guy handing out flyers on the street and supporting die-ins at the world's largest financial institutions. I was also a part of my company's green team and my town's sustainability group. I've volunteered with environmental organizations, phone banked for climate champions, spoken up at city council meetings, and worked to continuously minimize my family's carbon footprint.

I did all of this not because I'm an environmentalist or because I "found my passion" but because I believe the planetary emergency is the greatest challenge humanity has ever faced. And I believe that every one of us can help solve it – we *all* have something important to contribute.

I'm pretty good at learning, connecting dots, and writing (from the heart) in a way that inspires and empowers people to live more aligned with who they want to be – to make the positive impact they want to make.

That's why I wrote the newsletter. And that's why I wrote this book.

There are *billions* of good people like you who want to do more on climate. And I want to share the best practices, strategies, and resources I know of to help you walk this challenging, but rewarding path.

But before we dive into all of that, let me just say *thank you*. None of us chose to inherit this broken, collapsing system. But we are the ones who are here now at this pivotal moment in time. We are needed. *You* are needed. And I appreciate you for having the heart and courage to roll up your sleeves and rise to the challenge.

What You'll Get From This Book

Whether you are new to climate action, a seasoned veteran, or somewhere in between, this book will help you take the next steps on your climate journey. Here's the breakdown:

Part 1: Understanding the Situation

We'll start by diving into what the climate and ecological crisis means for society and why it matters. Then, because facing this reality is painful, we'll explore why our challenging eco-emotions arise and how to navigate our relationship with them in healthier ways. Once we feel a bit more grounded, we'll walk through what the world needs to do and the existing solutions we have to get the job done. Next, we'll take stock of the positive trends that are wind in our sails, because it's important to look not only at how far we have to go, but also at *how far we've come* – and what we have going for us. Finally, we'll paint a picture of a better future so we see not just what we're *against*, but also what we're *for* – giving us a north star to move toward.

Part 2: Your Power to Change Systems

This is my favorite section. It's all about understanding your power and how change works. It's easy to feel small and overwhelmed because the problem is so big. But this section shows you your power by highlighting the connection between our individual actions and systemic change. You'll learn how small groups of committed people have historically transformed societies (even when everyone thought it was impossible), how much your actions influence the people around you, and how you – as one of the few people who belongs to your specific communities and organizations – are needed to make change. After reading this, you'll never again wonder if what you do makes a difference.

Part 3: What You Can Do: Top 10 Effective Actions

This one's all about action. The first chapter will help you find your way by clarifying the direction and next steps that make the most sense for you to take on your climate journey. The next ten chapters serve as a menu of effective actions you can choose from (feel free to skip around!). You'll find many ways you can increase your positive impact, like learning how to talk about climate with others more easily and productively, making your community, company, or school more sustainable, finding a job in climate, minimizing your footprint, getting your money aligned, getting into activism, and electing climate champions. For every action, you'll learn why it matters and get a "how to" that gives you the tactics and tools you need to get started.

Part 4: On Moving Forward Wisely

This one is short and sweet. But there's no sugar-coating it – the road ahead of us will be challenging. So I want to focus on a few key intangibles to help you as you move forward on your climate journey: self-care, community, better stories, and always remembering what matters most.

As you can see, we'll cover a lot of ground in this book. But we won't cover everything. I tried to keep it as short as possible and share what I know best given my research, perspective, and experiences. There are many things I didn't include that I'd have liked to. And some that

I mention but don't go into more detail on. I hope you appreciate the book for what it is and find much of what it does cover useful. Where you see gaps, I hope you fill them in with your own climate action.

A final note on reading this book: while it's designed to be read from start to finish, each chapter also stands well on its own. So if, for example, you find yourself resisting reading about our dire situation in Chapter 1 (understandable), I encourage you to skip it and get to what's most relevant to you rather than putting the book down. Because you picked it up for a reason.

This is the guide I wish I had. I hope it helps you to take more effective actions, while making your life better all around. I hope you refer back to it over time. And, above all, I hope it gives you whatever it is that *you* need right now on your climate journey.

PART 1:
Understanding the Situation

1. The Big Picture

Let's start with a story:

> *There are these two young fish swimming along and they happen to meet an older fish swimming the other way, who nods at them and says, "Morning, boys. How's the water?"*
>
> *The two young fish swim on for a bit, and then eventually, one of them looks over at the other and goes, "**What the hell is water?**"*

As David Foster Wallace explained, "The point of the fish story is merely that the most obvious, important realities are often the ones that are hardest to see and talk about…so hidden in plain sight all around us, all the time, that we have to keep reminding ourselves over and over: This is water. This is water."

One of the most important realities to understand right now is this: we rely on our climate and ecosystems *for everything*. This is our water.

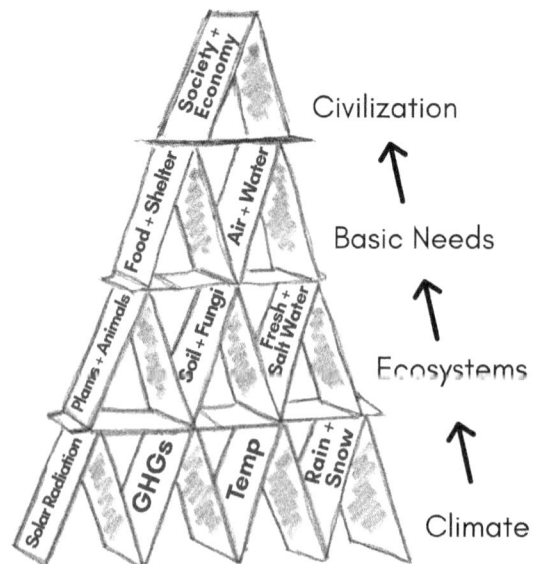

Foundations of Civilization. Illustrated by Kāya Pulz

Let's start with the basics. At the most fundamental level, we need air, water, and food to survive. You can't live more than a few minutes without air, a few days without water, or a few weeks without food.

If you're lucky, you may take these basic needs for granted. You go to the grocery store – the shelves are full of food. You turn on the faucet – water comes out. You breathe without thinking about it at all.

But our air, food, and water don't just magically appear out of nowhere. They come from **Earth's ecosystems**. (This is why cultures from around the world have called our planet *Mother* Earth for millennia – because Earth gives us life.)

Take plants, for example. Plants do two miraculous things for us. They make the air we breathe and the food we eat. We can't turn carbon dioxide into oxygen. Nor can we turn sunlight into food. We need plants to do these things for us. We *depend* on them.

Plants, in turn, depend on other beings in their ecosystem to survive, like fungi, insects, and tiny organisms in the soil – as well as having the climatic conditions they evolved in. They're just one example of *many* in this interdependent web of life we exist in.

So, although we don't talk about it much, healthy ecosystems and a stable climate are the foundations on which civilization was built. They are the context in which everything takes place. And we rely on them for all of our most basic needs: the food we eat, the water we drink, the air we breathe, the safety of our homes, our livelihoods, and a functioning economy.

These are the building blocks of society.

This is water.

But this water is getting *hot*.

Global Heating & Our Current Trajectory

Unfortunately, the stable climate and ecosystems we rely on for our basic needs are changing rapidly. The climate is changing faster than it has in millions of years – ten times faster, even, than it did during Earth's deadliest mass extinction event.

That's because our fossil-fuel-powered, habitat-destroying, growth-at-all-costs economic system is completely out of sync with the natural world it exists in. For all the innovation and progress it has made, the reality is that it's in the process of cutting off the hand that feeds it (Mother Earth's). The planet is becoming less and less habitable because the side effects of this system are destroying ecosystems and changing the composition of the atmosphere.

Since the industrial revolution, we've pumped 2.6 trillion tonnes of CO_2 into the atmosphere. Nature has worked overtime to absorb 56% of these emissions, but what remains has still increased atmospheric CO_2 by a whopping 50%. This blanket of greenhouse gases is the biggest thing humans have ever created – outweighing all of our buildings, roads, and products combined. It's also bigger than the shrinking mass of all life on Earth (e.g., populations of birds, fish, mammals, and reptiles have declined by 73% since 1970).

The result? This blanket has heated the Earth by about 1.4°C (2.6°F). Conservative estimates (that don't account for tipping points) put us on track for about 2.7°C (4.9°F) of heating by 2100, with the range going up to 3.4°C.

Why This Matters

It's tempting to think of this 2.7°C (4.9°F) of extra heat as a slightly warmer day. But a better way to think about it is to imagine how you would feel if your *body temperature* went up by 2.7°C (4.9°F). That's a 39.7°C fever (103.5°F).

If you had a fever that high, you'd be bedridden. If you had this fever for more than a few days (Earth's systems will have hotter temperatures for decades or centuries), you'd be on your way to the hospital. Your body wouldn't be able to function like it normally does.

It's also worth noting that the consequences of heating are *nonlinear*. If your fever doubled from 2.7°C to 5.4°C (a 42.4°C or 108.3°F fever) and you weren't able to cool down quickly enough, you wouldn't be twice as sick – you'd be having seizures, organ failure, permanent brain damage...or you'd be dead.

The bottom line is that this seemingly small amount of global heating that's already happened (1.4°C) means Earth's climate, weather, and ecosystems are no longer functioning like they have been for thousands of years. We're all seeing it with our own eyes now. With each year that passes, there are more extreme droughts, floods, wildfires, hurricanes, storms, jet streams, and heatwaves. And, like our bodies, Earth's systems will have nonlinear reactions as it gets hotter.

For decades, scientists have been warning that this level of planetary heating would be catastrophic for humanity. From President Lyndon B. Johnson's scientific advisors *in 1965* and Exxon's scientists in the 1970s, to Carl Sagan and James Hansen's testimonies to Congress in the 1980s, climate scientists have been sounding the alarm.

> *"Civilisation could prove a fragile thing."*
> **CONFIDENTIAL SHELL REPORT, 1989**

And they were right. They were right because the climate that was stable for thousands of years – the climate that allowed civilization to start in the first place – is long gone.

We have now heated the Earth past the safe range of temperatures that civilization was built in and designed for.

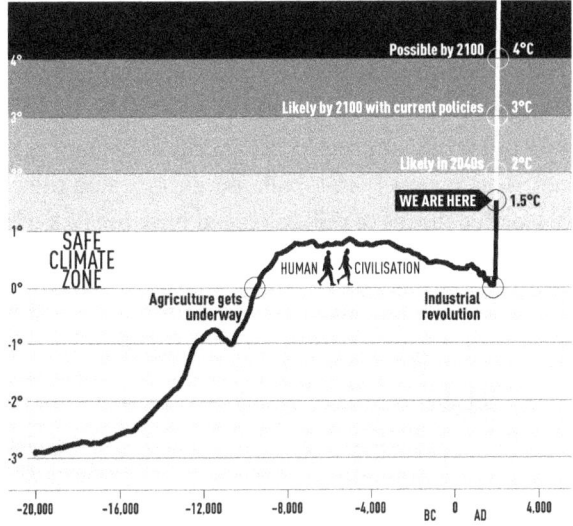

We've skyrocketed out of the safe climate zone. Credit: "Don't Mention the Emergency?" report, Morton 2020. Based on a chart by Jos Hagalaars. Data from multiple scientific papers.

Today's plants, animals, and ecosystems evolved **in** and **for** climatic conditions *that no longer exist*. These are the beings we rely on for the *food we eat* and the *air we breathe*. And for many of these beings, the climatic changes are happening so fast that it makes adaptation difficult or impossible, especially when combined with chemical pollution and habitat destruction.

Our homes, agriculture, infrastructure, supply chains, and economy were also built in and for climatic conditions *that no longer exist*.

So the foundations of civilization are getting weaker by the day. And because everything exists in a web of interdependence, when things stop working in one place, it often has consequences on other seemingly unrelated parts of the system.

Let's revisit the house of cards analogy and look at how climate chaos threatens each of our most basic needs:

Safe Places to Live

A staggering number of homes are located in places that were once considered safe but now face increasing risks.

Historically, most of the world's cities were built on coastlines for resources and trading purposes. The people who built them assumed the ocean wouldn't, you know, move in permanently. But the last time there was this much CO_2 in the atmosphere was over 3 million years ago. Back then temperatures were 1.9°C to 3.6°C hotter than preindustrial levels, and sea levels were 5 to 25 meters higher (16 to 82 feet). This means homes and communities on the coast (collectively worth trillions of dollars) are at growing risk of flooding and more intense hurricanes.

Meanwhile, inland areas face their own threats: wildfires, water scarcity, deadly heat, flooding, tornadoes, and more.

The ripple effects of this are starting to spread through our economic systems. As insurance companies re-evaluate these rising risks, they jack up their prices or stop offering coverage altogether (as has been happening in California and Florida). This means people have less money or can't afford to stay in their homes. It also means declining property values, which reduces tax revenue for local governments. So the towns that need to invest the most in climate adaptation will have less money to do so.

Food Security

Our food system, entirely dependent on ecosystems and climate, is becoming increasingly fragile. Habitat destruction, climate change, and pesticides continue to devastate the bees, butterflies, and beetles that pollinate our crops. Fewer pollinators means less food and higher prices. Increasing floods, fires, heat, drought, and expanding pest ranges in a warmer world also threaten supply. What you can grow and where you can grow it is changing.

These converging crises put the world's major food-producing regions at risk. From the American Midwest to Ukraine to China, extreme weather is already disrupting production in regions that feed billions of people. Scientists project that yields of staple crops like corn, wheat, and rice will decline in most places as the climate gets hotter and more chaotic. Not to mention chocolate, coffee, and alcohol. Or the 2.5 billion people who depend on farming for their livelihoods.

And don't forget the ocean. About 3 billion people rely on seafood as a major source of protein. But a hotter and more acidic ocean, combined with overfishing, fertilizer runoff, and plastic waste threatens the base of the food chain.

Clean Air

People who live in or near wildfire country know the smoke is no joke. Forest fires are burning twice as much land now as they did two decades ago, and the air pollution can be debilitating. About one-third of people in the US now live in counties considered "high risk" or "very high risk."

Less obvious connections matter too. More heat makes ground-level ozone worse. There are fewer plants (our oxygen producers) due to deforestation, wildfires, and desertification. And phytoplankton, tiny ocean creatures that supply more than half of the world's oxygen, are struggling in hotter, more acidic waters.

Fresh Water Supply

People rely on the consistency of their water sources, but this too is changing. Global heating threatens water security through more intense droughts, more evaporation, and changing rainfall patterns. Cape Town and Mexico City nearly ran out of water in recent years due to extended droughts combined with mismanagement. The Colorado River faces similar challenges. Its flows have declined by 20% since 2000 and are expected to go down another 20% to 35% by 2050.

About 60% of the world's freshwater flows come from mountains. The Himalayas, for example, act as "water towers" that provide freshwater for nearly two billion people. But global heating is disrupting these systems. Snow is melting earlier and faster, meaning less water is available later during dry seasons when it's most needed. And glaciers are also melting rapidly, with their contribution to river flows expected to decline significantly in the years ahead.

Meanwhile, coastal freshwater supplies face another threat: contamination from saltwater as sea levels rise and storms intensify.

This is just a fraction of the escalating impacts on our basic needs and how they cascade into each other. We didn't even get into people's livelihoods, like the 2.4 billion outdoor workers who are increasingly impacted by heat waves, forced to make impossible choices between a paycheck and their safety. Or how extreme weather is causing more and longer power outages, which can be deadly (like in Puerto Rico or Texas). Or health impacts – like how disease-spreading ticks and mosquitoes are expanding their ranges to new places and global pandemics are increasingly likely.

When these basic needs decrease, it means life gets harder. It means prices go up. It means people are forced to leave their homes because it's not safe or they can't get by there anymore. It means instability, uncertainty, and increased conflict and violence. It means people die. That's why these are the building blocks of civilization. We need them to function. And to have enough of them, we need a stable climate and healthy ecosystems.

It's also important to understand that climate change isn't the only issue. It's just one of nine planetary boundaries that scientists have identified as critical for Earth's life-support systems. We briefly touched on some of the others above (e.g., habitat destruction, biodiversity loss, pollution, freshwater use, ocean acidification). We're now exceeding the safe limits on seven of the planetary boundaries. These interconnected issues are all part of the same story: we're pushing our planet beyond its limits to support us.

Simply put, our civilization now exists in an increasingly extreme environment that it was not designed for. And behind all these stats are the impacts they are having on *real people's lives*.

Beyond Statistics: The Human Cost

To be honest, it's impossible for any of us to wrap our heads around the full extent of what this means. We're in uncharted territory.

Perhaps the most important thing to understand is that climate and ecological breakdown are making the world less habitable. There are a lot of people living in places today that will soon be too hard to live in. In 2024, a record-high of 45 million people were forced to leave their homes by disasters like storms, floods, wildfires, and drought. That's more than 1 person every second. This number is expected to grow to hundreds of millions of people by 2050 – possibly over 1 billion – when slower-moving climate impacts like sea level rise are also accounted for.

But these statistics don't translate to what this actually *means*. A story may start to though. Here's one I'll never forget. It's about a 14-year-old girl named Pakhi. Her family lived in rural Bangladesh. In 2014, they lost their home in a massive flood. They lost everything and didn't have enough money to get by. So Pakhi, along with hundreds of thousands of others, moved to the closest city, Dhaka. Once there, she became a sex worker to support her parents and younger siblings. Four years later, she explained, "I did it only for the money. I had to buy food. I had to survive…The flood took everything away from us by destroying our house. We are in this situation because of the flood." Unfortunately, this story isn't unique. When poverty gets so extreme, it's not uncommon for girls to be forced into work they don't want to do or be married off at extremely young ages.

Climate events can also destabilize entire regions. In 2011, a civil war broke out in Syria. There were many factors that made it a tinderbox. One of them was a 1-in-500-year drought from 2006 to 2011 (the worst ever recorded there). This killed crops and livestock, leading to food shortages and malnutrition. It made water scarce. Poverty went up alongside prices, making it hard for people to get by. Kids were forced to drop out of school and find work. This led 1.5 million people to migrate from rural areas to already overcrowded cities and was a key driver of social unrest leading up to the war. The war was one of the most devastating and disruptive since World War II, with more than 600,000 people killed and 13 million displaced (half of the country).

These stories are heartbreaking. They're also why what we choose to do about the planetary emergency matters so much. Every action we take, every policy or investment we influence, every fraction of a degree we prevent makes life better not just for people in your community but for people around the world.

Again, this is all about the building blocks of society: having enough food to eat, water to drink, clean air to breathe, safe places to live, and jobs that help us get by. Our systems are not prepared for the climatic changes that have already occurred, never mind what the future has in store as the effects get worse and cascade into each other.

What will happen to the global food system in the face of decreasing crop yields due to extreme floods, drought, heat, soil degradation, and fewer pollinators? What happens if pandemics and insect-borne illnesses increase as expected? What will happen to marine ecosystems that are the main protein source for billions of people as the ocean continues to heat up and become more acidic? What will the cities that are on track to run out of water in the coming years do? How high will sea levels rise and how quickly – how many homes and cities will they take off the map? How many millions or billions of people will be forced to leave their homes? What happens if crucial ecosystems that sequester large amounts of carbon collapse?

And what happens if we cross a tipping point in Earth's system? These are self-reinforcing feedback loops that, at some point, become unstoppable. A classic example is the Greenland ice sheet: as white ice that reflects sunlight melts, it's replaced by dark water that *absorbs* sunlight. This, in turn, melts more ice. The fear is that crossing one of these tipping points could be like knocking over the first domino, setting off a chain reaction that leads to runaway heating.

Scientists have identified sixteen tipping points in Earth's system. We're already at risk of triggering five of them at current temperatures.

Estimated range of global heating needed to pass tipping point temperature

CURRENTLY IN DANGER ZONE	Greenland ice sheet collapse
	West Antarctic ice sheet collapse
	Tropical coral reef die-off
	Northern permafrost abrupt thaw
	Labrador Sea current collapse
DANGER ZONE WITHIN THE PARIS AGREEMENT RANGE	Barents Sea ice loss
	Mountain glaciers loss
	Atlantic current collapse
	Northern forests dieback · South
	Northern forests expansion · North
	West African monsoon shift
	East Antarctic glacier collapse
	Amazon rainforest dieback
	Northern permafrost collapse
	Arctic winter sea ice collapse
	East Antarctic ice sheet collapse

1.4°C Current level of warming — 1.5–2.0°C Paris agreement targets
MIN — RANGE — MAX • CENTRAL ESTIMATE
Source: Armstrong McKay et al, Science, 2022.

These are the tipping points. Avoiding them is kiiind of essential. Credit: PIK & GLOBAÏA (modified). Data: Armstrong McKay et al, Science, 2022.

The honest answer is we don't know what the future holds or how bad things will get. But it's undeniable that the current trajectory for life on Earth is terrifying. And you don't have to take that from me – take it from the people who understand these life-support systems better than anyone else – climate scientists and ecologists:

> *"If we carry on the way we are going now, I can't see this civilization lasting to the end of this century – no chance in my view on the current trajectory."*
>
> TIM LENTON, Director of Global Systems Institute

> "We are, without exaggeration, facing a trajectory and impacts that will obliterate the possibility of human civilization by the year 2100."
>
> JULIA K. STEINBERGER, IPCC Lead Author

Even if you disagree and think these experts (and many of their peers) are off by 50%, that's still a very dark path to be on.

This is why we must change our trajectory.

This is why the planetary emergency is the greatest challenge of our time.

And this is why climate action is really about something we all fundamentally care about: protecting the people and places we love.

There is so much worth fighting for. And so much we can still save if enough of us decide to consistently show up and do something about it, *together*.

You may have noticed challenging emotions arise while reading this chapter. That's because facing the reality of what's going on in our world is not easy – it's scary and painful. Maybe you even thought about putting the book down or had to mentally brace yourself before opening the book because you knew reading about how bad things are would be hard (I do this with climate stuff too, it's normal). But this avoidant instinct points to a crucial and often overlooked point: There are big psychological barriers to even *thinking* about climate, never mind *doing* something about it. And it's not just you – climate and ecological breakdown are causing a mental health crisis around the world.

That's why the next chapter is about helping you face and navigate this emotionally challenging terrain more easily – both for your mental health and so you have more energy to take action.

> "Not everything that is faced can be changed. But nothing can be changed unless it is faced."
>
> JAMES BALDWIN, writer and civil rights activist

2. Getting Grounded: Navigating Eco-Emotions

We are presented with one overarching question: Are we going to let our feelings overrun and deplete us, or are we going to use our feelings to overrun the systems that are making us so unwell?
DR. BRITT WRAY, *Generation Dread*

I don't know about you, but the planetary crisis makes me feel SO many different things.

Sometimes I'm scared or anxious.

What does climate and ecological breakdown mean for people around the world and life on Earth? What does it mean for me, my loved ones, our homes, and our future? Are we going to be okay?

Sometimes I'm filled with grief.

There is and will be so much suffering. How many people, plants, and animals are going to needlessly suffer or die?

Sometimes I get pissed off.

The fossil fuel industry actively spent billions of dollars to steer us down this deadly path despite knowing it'd harm billions of people. How is that okay? And how do they still get subsidies and have so much power in 2025? Will there ever be consequences for their crime against humanity?

Sometimes I feel cynical.

Politicians are in the pockets of the world's biggest corporations. And corporations care about their bottom line above all else. Will enough leaders in the world's biggest governments and corporations ever act at the speed and scale that this crisis requires?

Sometimes I feel tired.

I'm just overwhelmed by it all. It's so big. There's so much to do. And I'm just me.

Why Our Eco-Emotions are Normal and Useful

It's important to understand that these are all completely normal and healthy reactions to the situation we find ourselves in. And that you are not alone in experiencing these emotions.

In fact, these feelings are simply a sign that you are human. It means you have a caring heart, a functioning brain, and that you're aware of what's going on around you.

Learning about the reality of the climate crisis and the destruction of ecological systems can bring up these emotions because our bodies and brains correctly interpret this information as threats to our well-being and survival.

These eco-emotions may not feel good, but they're doing the job they *evolved* to do: keeping us alive. They're providing us with useful feedback on the information we're receiving about the environmental and social systems we exist in and rely on. They're trying to tell us that what is happening in these systems is dangerous to our present and future well-being. They're trying to give us the nudge we need to take actions that will help keep us alive.

And yet, despite working as designed, these emotions often fail to accomplish their goals. They are often suppressed immediately – outmatched by our brains' speedy, well-practiced psychological defenses.

Spectrum of Denial

Whether conscious or not, on some level, we know that we are a part of these ecological systems that are breaking down and that we rely on them for everything.

But even though these are hugely important issues (or, likely, it's *because* they're so big), many of us turn away from these challenging emotions and thoughts as soon as they come up – avoiding them every time because they're painful.

Naomi Klein has an eye-opening passage in her book *This Changes*

Everything on how, even if you know climate change is real, looking away from it every time it pops into your head with one rationalization or another is actually a form of denial:

> "I denied climate change for longer than I care to admit. I knew it was happening, sure. Not like Donald Trump and the Tea Partiers going on about how the continued existence of winter proves it's all a hoax. But I stayed pretty hazy on the details and only skimmed most of the news stories, especially the really scary ones. I told myself the science was too complicated and that the environmentalists were dealing with it. And I continued to behave as if there was nothing wrong. … A great many of us engage in this kind of climate change denial. We look for a split second and then we look away. … We deny because we fear that letting in the full reality of this crisis will change everything. And we are right."

Denial is one of the stages of grief. And when it comes to climate, most of us are on a spectrum of denial. Just as our emotions evolved to help protect us, our brain's reaction to these challenging emotions is also an attempt to be protective.

As Dr. Britt Wray writes, "For the majority among us, it's not that we outright deny that this crisis is happening. But we turn away from its terrifying implications in order to protect ourselves from the anxiety it causes and resist the changes that are necessary but uncomfortable to make."

So this "soft" denial is *also* a defense mechanism (albeit a conflicting one) that ends up suppressing the alarm bells of our distressing emotions.

It's almost like our emotions are saying "HEY, this is a threat – feels like a big deal. We should probably do something about this." And then our brain and nervous system are like "HEY, this anxiety doesn't feel good. Plus acting on this information would mean change and uncertainty…and we don't like those things. So, let's pass for now."

At times, this "looking for a split second and then looking away" is useful. It helps us get on with our days and do what we need to do. But if we never actually let ourselves fully look at, feel, and process these emotions – if we don't let ourselves face the reality of our situation – it becomes highly problematic. This way of being is unhealthy and unhelpful both for us and the greater whole we're a part of.

> "The refusal to feel takes a heavy toll. Not only is there an impoverishment of our emotional and sensory life, flowers are dimmer and less fragrant, our loves less ecstatic, but this psychic numbing also impedes our capacity to process and respond to information. The energy expended in pushing down despair is diverted from more creative uses, depleting the resilience and imagination needed for fresh visions and strategies."
>
> JOANNA MACY, author, scholar, activist

This brings us to the question: instead of suppressing and denying these eco-emotions, what *should* we do? How do we navigate them in a healthier and more helpful way?

Strategies and Resources for Navigating Eco-Emotions

I think Dr. Elizabeth Sawin put it well when she said, "Honor your difficult feelings. You're an animal whose life-support system is in danger. It would be really weird to not be afraid or to not be furious about that. There's intelligence in those feelings. Feel them, but don't let them paralyze you. Let them move through and take them as information."

Rather than looking away from your difficult emotions, it's important to face and process them (at least sometimes). Here are some simple steps that might help:

1. **Pause and decide to face the feeling**

    When you notice an eco-emotion arise, stop what you're doing and take a deep breath. Decide to face it rather than suppress it.

2. **"Name it to tame it"**
   Figure out which feeling it is. Is it fear? Grief? Anger? Overwhelm? When you name the emotion, some of its power goes away. This isn't just a trick – neuroscience tells us that naming our emotions can calm us down.

3. **Feel it in your body and breathe**
   Where do you feel the emotion? Is it a knot in your stomach? Tension in your neck or shoulders? Tightness in your chest? Breathe deeply into that area – let it soften.

4. **Embrace it with compassion**
   Talk to the emotion (yes, really). Treat it like you would a friend. "Welcome anxiety. It makes sense you're here. You're paying attention to what's going on and what it means for our future. Thank you." Be kind, understanding, and accept it.

5. **Connect it to what you care about**
   Your emotion is trying to help you. So ask: "Why are you here – what are you trying to help me with? What is it about this that I really care about?"

This emotional processing takes time and space. It takes courage and vulnerability. It means being open and honest with yourself.

I know it might sound strange if you haven't done it before. But, in my experience (as the king of suppressing emotions), it's 100% worth it. When you let yourself feel, name, and breathe into your challenging emotions, it takes some of their power away. As you become more familiar with the emotions, you get better at integrating them when they arise, rather than suppressing them. And when you've listened to them and understand why they're arising, you can start to reinvest that energy you were using to suppress them into a more positive response. Maybe you share what you were feeling with a friend. Maybe you journal about it to get more clarity. Maybe you commit to taking a climate action that will help address the root cause of the emotion. This action, in turn, can help reduce the frequency with which your challenging emotions arise because you are actively doing something about it. Or, maybe, in that moment, you just need to rest – trust yourself!

Remember: processing your eco-emotions isn't a one-time thing. These feelings will keep arising, and that's okay. But each time you practice these steps, you build emotional resilience and reconnect with your core values.

As Dr. Britt Wray says, "We need to find a balance in this matrix of feelings. The sweet spot, where we're not just intellectually engaged with the crisis but also emotionally engaged. A place where we know how to integrate the dark emotions into our lives so that when they appear we don't fall apart. Where we're in touch with our care for the world instead of numbed by our unconscious defenses. And where we're able to aim for something more and see ourselves as being able to make a difference, knowing that what we do matters even if it is small. All of this requires a high degree of emotional intelligence. We have to practice it and we need support to do so because it is not innate to all of us."

I've written before that action is the antidote to despair. But action alone is not enough. According to Wray, the true antidote to despair is acknowledging your feelings, connecting with others who feel them, and taking aligned action. As we do this, we strengthen our relationship with ourselves, nature, and the people around us.

So share your feelings and this process with people in your life. Processing eco-emotions together is far more powerful than doing it alone. If you'd like to have more structure or community around this, I'd highly recommend you check out:

- The Work That Reconnects: workshops on grief, gratitude, and action
- We Are the Great Turning podcast: created for group discussions and exercises
- The All We Can Save Project's Circles: community, dialogue, and action
- The Good Grief Network: 10-week programs for processing climate emotions

And for ongoing support.

- The Unthinkable Newsletter, resource hub, and Generation Dread by Britt Wray
- Eco-Anxious Stories
- Project Inside Out (especially for organizations)

At first glance, this emotional work might seem separate from climate action. But it just might be the key to unlocking the mass action we need.

Why Emotions are Key to Accelerating Climate Action

This emotional work is healthy, beneficial, and worth doing in its own right.

But we're also facing a planetary emergency right now – an all-hands-on-deck situation. And despite a majority of people being alarmed or concerned about the climate crisis, there's still only a tiny fraction of people acting in alignment with those beliefs.

There are hundreds of millions of people who may start investing more time into climate action if they truly let themselves engage with and process these deep and painful emotions. So encouraging and facilitating this emotional work is a massive, untapped, win-win opportunity. The suppression and denial of difficult eco-emotions could very well be a dam holding back a surge of climate action.

And right now we need a lot more people working on this problem. So, though it's rarely discussed, engaging with our emotions is key to accelerating climate action.

We are all capable of learning how to handle these emotions in a healthy way. And it's worth remembering that in doing so, we will bring more love, connection, and belonging into our lives.

Other Things I Feel

Not *all* my eco-emotions are challenging.

Sometimes I feel hopeful.

Like when I meet new people in the space doing amazing things, learn about another reader I inspired to act in a big way, or when I see action accelerating around the world.

Sometimes I feel determined.

I know that things are bad and that they're going to get worse before they can get better. But I also know that we can always help make things better than they otherwise would be. I know that what I do makes a difference. And I want to help make the world a better place. So, regardless of how things turn out, I am going to do my best. Even if we do go down, I would rather go down swinging.

Sometimes I feel love.

In fact, I believe that love is the driving emotion behind nearly all the other eco-emotions. I'm feeling all of these things because I love the world. I am a part of it. And the climate crisis is putting people, beings, and places I love at risk.

If we explore how love connects to the other eco-emotions we're experiencing, I believe it can unleash enormous amounts of well-being and action.

Because love is the most powerful emotion of all.

> *"Pain is useful. Don't be afraid of it. If you're afraid of it, you won't know where it comes from. It comes from love. And love is what is going to pull us through."*
>
> JOANNA MACY

Our eco-emotions will continue to arise. That's just part of being an aware and caring human right now. My hope is that this chapter and the resources in it help you improve your relationship with these emotions moving forward. And I hope it helps you clarify your *why* – understanding why they're happening and why this all matters so much to you. If you take some time to work on this, you may notice a positive side effect in addition to better mental health: you'll have more energy and determination to act on climate.

Which is great. Because there's a lot of good work that needs doing!

3. What the World Needs to Do

In a world on fire, stop burning things.
                    BILL MCKIBBEN, author and activist

In the Paris Agreement, the world agreed to limit global heating to well below 2°C and to aim for 1.5°C because 2°C…would be awful. Island nations say "1.5 to stay alive" for good reason.

It's estimated that to have a chance of limiting heating to 1.5°C by 2100 would require cutting emissions in half by 2030 and getting to net-zero emissions globally by 2050.

As of 2025, we've heated the planet by 1.4°C and are on track for ~2.7°C under current policies. But every fraction of a degree of heating we can prevent matters. And how hot it gets is still largely up to us as far as we know.

So, at a high level, our goal is pretty simple:

Stop *global heating, and* **start** *bringing temperatures back down to safer levels as quickly, safely, and equitably as possible.*

To accomplish this, we need to achieve "drawdown." As Chad Frischmann, a Co-Creator of Project Drawdown says, "Drawdown is that point in time when we *take out* more greenhouse gases than we *put into* Earth's atmosphere."

This is the first step to get back toward the safer temperatures that our life-support systems evolved in and our infrastructure was designed for. And the faster we do this, the better off we will be. The question of course is *how*.

To answer this, we'll lean on Project Drawdown's pioneering framework on climate solutions, developed by the original team of 100+ scientists and researchers.

Reduce Sources, Support Sinks, and Improve Society

Here's Project Drawdown's three-pronged framework for climate solutions:

1. Reduce Sources: bringing emissions to zero
2. Support Sinks: uplifting nature's carbon cycle
3. Improve Society: fostering equality for all

So, first and foremost, we need to stop making the problem worse. That means working to get society's 57 billion tonnes of annual greenhouse gas emissions to *zero* as quickly as we can. About 75% of emissions come from burning fossil fuels. So an easy rule of thumb is to stop burning fossil fuels. The remaining ~25% of emissions are from food, agriculture, deforestation, and industrial processes.

Here's a breakdown of where these emissions are coming from:

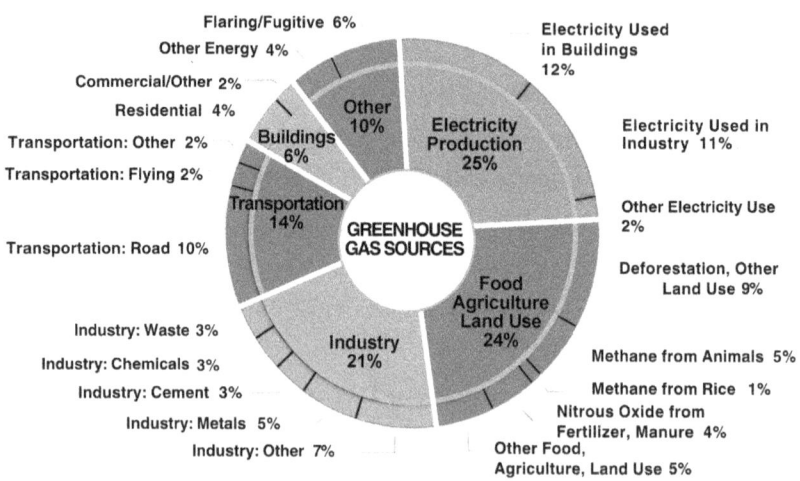

Global emissions by sector. Credit: Project Drawdown

Second, we need to support nature's land and ocean sinks. Thankfully, nature has been removing 41% of the greenhouse gas emissions society puts up into the atmosphere (think: plants sequestering CO_2). This is extremely important. We need to do everything we can to protect and support these natural carbon sinks because their capacity to keep lifting this massive load is declining. And we need to sequester hundreds of billions of tonnes of emissions from the atmosphere (even after we get to net-zero) to get back to safe levels.

Third, we need to improve society. When we do good by people, we generally do good by climate. When we stand up with Indigenous communities and protect their rights, they are able to live well and take care of the ecosystems where they live – which is where most of the world's remaining biodiversity is found. When we advance human rights like education and reproductive freedom, especially for girls and women, health and opportunities flourish – as educated women with access to family planning tend to earn more and have fewer and healthier children – which in turn grows gender equality and reduces emissions.

Here are the specific solutions within each pillar of this three-pronged framework and the size of their emission reduction potential:

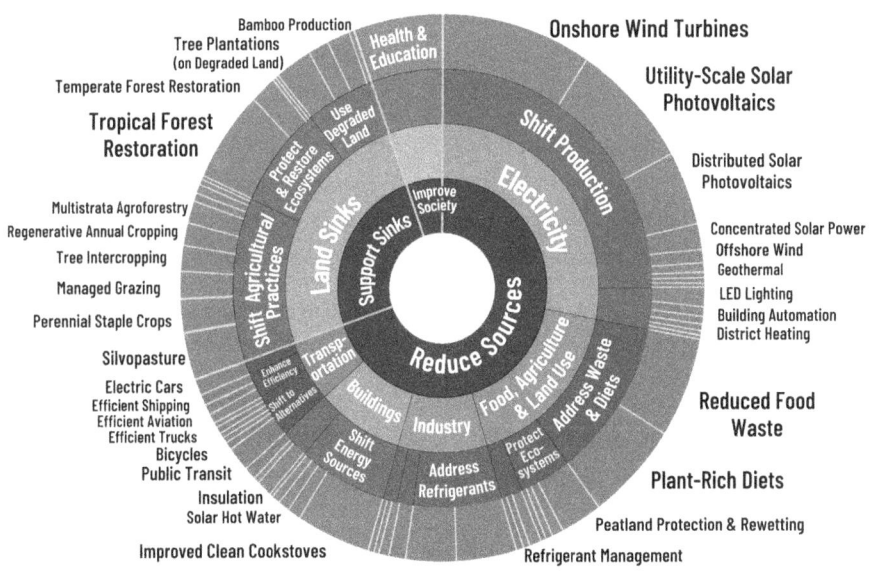

Climate solutions. Credit: Project Drawdown (modified)

According to Project Drawdown's research, we can hit our temperature targets if we implement these solutions by 2050. They estimate that limiting heating to 2°C would cost $22 trillion more than we'd otherwise spend and would lead to $95 trillion in operational savings, while 1.5°C would cost $28 trillion and save $145 trillion. According to the Climate Policy Initiative, this translates to a total investment of $6 trillion into climate solutions annually (compared to the $2 trillion being invested right now).

To oversimplify and summarize the solutions in this framework, here's what we need to do:

- Protect and restore ecosystems
- Increase efficiency and reduce unnecessary consumption
- Electrify all our machines that run on fossil fuels
- Power everything with 100% clean energy
- Switch to regenerative agricultural practices
- Advance education and reproductive freedom for girls and women
- Eat less meat and waste less food
- Move to a circular economy with zero waste
- Research and scale the technology needed to eliminate the last ~20% of emissions (e.g., pollution-free planes, cement, steel, etc.)

(Two more things to keep in mind. Putting a price on carbon, like Citizens' Climate Lobby's Carbon Fee & Dividend proposal, would accelerate all of this. And rewiring democracies so that representatives are responsive to citizens rather than special interests is also key.)

The good news is **we already have most of the solutions we need to do this**. And they're economical.

The bad news is we have to implement all these solutions faster than we've done pretty much anything else, ever. Because unlike most issues, time is not on our side when it comes to solving the climate crisis.

Cut Emissions ASAP

Every day that goes by, our destructive systems dump more heat-trapping gases into the atmosphere that stay there for hundreds of years. The more fuel we add to the fire, the harder it gets for life on Earth. And the more likely we are to cross climatic or ecological tipping points that threaten to collapse civilization itself.

This is why the "time value of carbon" is a crucial concept to understand in the fight against climate change.

The Time Value of Carbon

You may have heard of "the time value of money." This refers to the fact that $100 today is worth more than $100 a year from now. That's because if you have the $100 today, you can invest it and have, say, $107 next year. So getting money today is more valuable than getting it next year because money grows over time.

Similarly, cutting emissions this year is more valuable than cutting emissions next year. This is because, like money, the value of early emission cuts grows over time. For example, let's say your city emits 1 million tonnes of greenhouse gas emissions annually from its fossil fuel-powered electricity. But after years of hard work, you and your fellow citizens get a policy passed that switches your city to 100% clean electricity.

This single action prevents an additional 1 million tonnes from entering the atmosphere – not only this year but every single year that follows. After five years, that's 5 million tonnes of pollution avoided. After twenty years, it's 20 million tonnes.

The point here is that every year matters. A lot. The longer we take to implement solutions, the more heat-trapping emissions pile up in the atmosphere.

Here's a visual illustrating how powerful the time value of carbon is on our path to net-zero. The solid line shows annual greenhouse gas emissions. The shaded area on the right shows the massive amount of emissions prevented by cuts made in different decades.

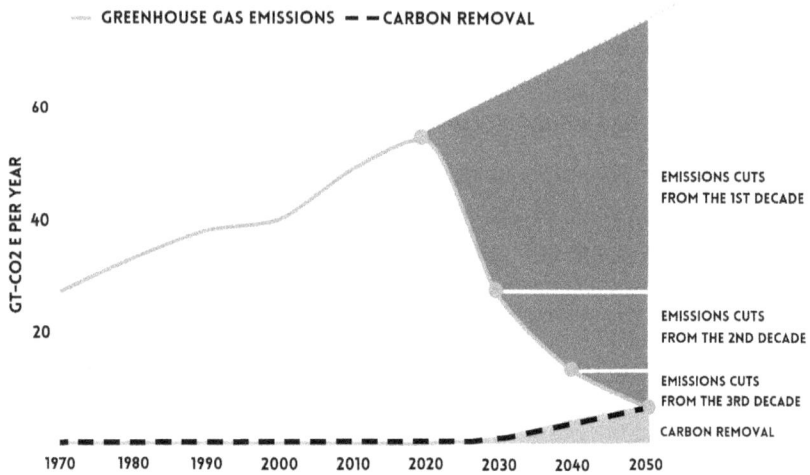

I share this to demonstrate the time value of carbon. To be clear, as of 2025, emissions are still going up. Credit: Project Drawdown.

As you can see, the earliest emission cuts have the biggest impact by far. In this example, emission cuts between 2020 and 2030 eliminate 76% of the total preventable emissions between now and 2050. In other words, these early emission cuts are 76% of the solution of how we get to net-zero by 2050. Emission cuts in the second decade eliminate about 18% of emissions. The third eliminates about 2% of emissions. And carbon removal is about 4% of the solution.

All in all, cutting emissions is 96% of what we need to do – and doing it early with the solutions that exist today is *extremely* important.

The faster we cut emissions, the better off we will be. And a huge part of this comes down to something simple: keeping most fossil fuels in the ground.

Keep It in the Ground

Let's be clear about something: we cannot burn the great majority of the fossil fuels that are in the ground. Burning all the fossil fuels would lead to 6.4°C to 9.5°C of heating and make the world unrecognizable.

This is why Mark Carney, the Prime Minister of Canada, said, "The vast majority of reserves are unburnable." Similarly, the (historically conservative) International Energy Agency said there cannot be any new exploration or development of fossil fuel resources if we want to meet our 1.5°C or 2°C targets.

In other words, it's time to stop building out new fossil fuel infrastructure. The science is clear: the mines and fields that we extract coal, oil, and gas from today need to be the last ones. But governments and corporations *aren't listening* to the science. They say one thing (pledge to meet Paris targets) while doing another (expanding fossil fuel production). Fossil fuel companies, and the banks, insurance companies, and governments that support them are still exploring and developing *new* fossil fuel fields and mines to extract from. They're still investing *hundreds of billions of dollars* into it every year.

According to the United Nations Environment Programme's "Production Gap Report," governments "still plan to produce more than double the amount of fossil fuels in 2030 than would be consistent with limiting warming to 1.5°C." This is mind-bogglingly stupid. Maintaining the status quo is deadly. We need to be managing a rapid decline in fossil fuel production, finding quick, safe, and equitable ways to keep as many fossil fuels in the ground as possible.

That's why the campaign for a Fossil Fuel Non-Proliferation Treaty is gaining steam. Its goal is to complement the Paris Agreement with a binding plan "to halt the expansion of fossil fuels, manage an equitable phase-out of coal, oil and gas, and lay the foundations for a just energy transition in which no worker, community or country is left behind."

Keeping trillions of dollars of fossil fuels in the ground is essential. It's also extremely difficult and will require many people to get on board. But this challenge becomes easier when we recognize an underappreciated truth: climate solutions don't only solve climate change – they also solve *a lot* of other problems people care about.

My favorite climate cartoon. Copyright: Joel Pett, reprinted with permission.

Multisolve

> "Multisolving is when you make a single investment, policy, or action that addresses multiple problems at the same time."
>
> **DR. ELIZABETH SAWIN**, Director at the Multisolving Institute

We've been taught to solve problems by breaking them down into smaller, more manageable pieces. But multisolving, based in systems thinking, takes a different approach. Instead of zooming in on a problem and its smaller components, multisolving shows us that a problem can get easier to solve when you zoom out and bundle it together with other problems.

For example, if you're trying to get your city off of fossil fuels to help solve climate change, it can help to zoom out and ask: who else is suffering from this?

When it comes to fossil fuels, you can quickly see that they are causing people to suffer for many reasons *beyond* causing climate change. The most obvious one is people suffering from air pollution. Air pollution from fossil fuels kills around 8.7 million people a year or nearly *1 out of every 5 people who die*, and takes over one year off everyone's life on average. The World Health Organization estimates that air pollution is responsible for 25% of deaths from heart disease, 43% of deaths from lung disease, 24% of deaths from strokes, 29% of deaths from lung cancer, and more. So if someone has any of these conditions, or loves someone who does, they probably also care about getting off of fossil fuels even if they don't care about climate change. The same goes for people who have cancer, Alzheimer's, asthma, etc. Or for soon to be parents and grandparents because the air pollution particles from fossil fuels are so small they can even get into the womb and harm babies before they're born.

Much like the impacts of climate change, this air pollution from burning fossil fuels disproportionately affects people of color and low-income communities. So solving these problems also increases environmental, social, and economic justice.

People also suffer from how much money fossil fuels cost them. This includes whoever pays for the medical bills of people suffering from pollution-related health issues – whether it's an employer, government, insurance company, or individuals and their families. And it also includes people who have a hard time paying expensive fossil fuel energy bills (e.g., electricity, heating, gasoline, etc.). Climate solutions can help all of these groups save money.

The same goes for local economies. Our communities collectively spend millions on fossil fuels – sending money to faraway corporations. But when we transition to clean, local energy, much of that money stays local, benefiting residents and small businesses.

When you start adding people's problems together like this, it gets easier to find other people who care about and will advocate for the solution because it solves many different people's problems at once. Everyone can get behind the solution for the reason that matters most to them, whether it's climate, health, justice, or their pocketbook. And that's the beauty of multisolving.

This problem-solving framework is also crucial for bigger systems like national governments. Though the public health savings from getting off of fossil fuels far outweigh the cost of the transition, these costs and benefits fall on siloed departments with separate budgets and balance sheets. For example, the transportation and energy departments are the ones that have to make all the big upfront investments to get off of fossil fuels, but it would be the health department that would see the savings most immediately as hospital visits go down. To be clear, the transportation and energy departments would also see savings over time. But the point is that the cost-benefit analysis of these decisions needs to be made across departments so upfront resources can be pooled, benefits can be shared, and the multisolving action can be implemented.

Nature-based solutions are also great examples of multisolving. Protecting and restoring coastal wetlands like salt marshes, seagrass, and mangroves benefits many people at once. Not only do these ecosystems mitigate climate change by sequestering carbon, but they also help protect coastal towns from flooding, sea level rise, and storms. Healthier coastal ecosystems can also lead to more seafood which increases food security and helps the local fishermen and economies that rely on them.

Multisolving is an elegant, inclusive, and effective way of thinking that we should apply to our work as much as possible. Everyone has reasons to care about and advocate for climate solutions, even if they don't care about the planetary emergency, because these solutions improve people's health, finances, and quality of life.

Identifying and collaborating with the full range of people whose problems can be solved by a single action is key to making these big changes more quickly and effectively!

Build Resilience & Prepare for Climate Chaos

This book mostly focuses on *mitigating* the climate crisis – to stop making it worse. That's because, if the problem gets too bad, adaptation becomes impossible. But given how bad things already are, and how much more heating is already locked in, we need to invest a lot more time, energy, and resources into increasing our resilience. We need to prepare our homes, communities, food systems, water systems, infrastructure, supply chains, and more for a future that is getting more extreme and unpredictable by the day.

So as we make policy and investment decisions to mitigate the planetary crisis, we should make sure they also build our resilience to its impacts. Likewise, our actions to build resilience should also help to mitigate the crisis.

This topic, as with most of these chapters, could be a book on its own. But I want to highlight this one in particular as absolutely crucial to keep top of mind as you go forward on your climate journey. Planetary breakdown is going to throw a lot at us. If we aren't at least somewhat prepared, we may not have the resources or social cohesion to solve the root of the problem.

Shift from "Less Bad" to "More Good"

When you put all of this together – when you realize just how much needs to happen and how little time we have to do it all – it becomes clear that what is generally accepted as "sustainable" today just isn't going to cut it. The goalpost needs to move.

Most corporations, governments, and individuals still think sustainability is simply a matter of reducing their footprint – of doing *less* bad.

That strategy may have worked 100 years ago when Earth's systems were healthier, more resilient, and more capable of supporting life. But our economic system has been harming Earth's systems for so long now that doing less bad or being neutral isn't good enough. True sustainability can't be achieved unless we repair the damage that's been done. In other words, we need to redesign our social and economic systems to *regenerate* Earth's systems rather than *degenerate* them. Regeneration is how we restore Earth's capacity to support life.

You can also think of this as having a net positive impact (accounting for the full ripple effect of actions). This regenerative, net positive impact is what I mean when I say "climate positive" and "planet positive species." It's about good impacts far outweighing any bad ones. And humans improving our relationship with the planet so that we start leaving things *better* than we found them, not just for ourselves and future generations, but for all the beings who live here.

If you only remember one thing, remember this: *we already have most of the solutions we need*. And they're not just climate solutions.

They can solve multiple problems at the same time, improving our health, economy, and nearly every other issue we care about. They will save the world trillions of dollars. And, most importantly, they will help save and improve billions of lives.

We know what we need to do. And if we get our act together in time, we can build a better world. A world where all life thrives.

That being said, the reality is that the gap between where we are today and that better world we want to live in is huge. It's easy to feel overwhelmed and fall into the trap of thinking that big changes are impossible and the status quo will never change. That's why it's crucial to recognize an often overlooked reality: we have made a ton of progress in recent years. To keep our spirits up and get to where we want to go, it's essential to occasionally look back at this progress – to ground ourselves in how far we've come and how much momentum we now have.

4. What We Have Going For Us

Shift the focus from what's wrong to what's strong, and build that strength to create a better tomorrow.

CORMAC RUSSELL, author of *Asset-Based Community Development*

Now, I understand there is a *huge* gap between the world as it is and the world that we want – between how fast we are taking action and how fast we need to be.

These gaps can be painful and disheartening. That's why it's important to not only think about what's wrong and how far we have to go but to also reflect on what we've got going for us and how far we've come. This practice can help us stay grounded, appreciate the progress we *have* made, evaluate what has been most effective, and see what strengths we can use to accelerate progress moving forward.

So, here's a look at the recent progress we've made and some of the positive, high-level trends that we have going for us:

Public Awareness and Demand for Action is Growing

- The climate and environmental movement is arguably the biggest movement in history. There has been an explosion of impactful climate activism since 2018. From the emergence of the Sunrise Movement to Greta Thunberg and Fridays for Future, Extinction Rebellion, and so many more – millions of people have taken to the streets to demand systemic change as quickly as possible.
- As of 2025, 67% of people around the world see climate change as a "major threat."
- A staggering 89% of people want their government to take more action.

Our Energy System is Transforming

- In 2020, the International Energy Agency announced that

solar was "the cheapest source of electricity in history." By 2024, solar and wind projects were cheaper than fossil fuels over 90% of the time, and 41% of the world's electricity came from zero-carbon sources.
- Battery storage costs have fallen by about 84% over the last ten years. This helps solve one of the biggest challenges for renewable energy – intermittency – while also making electric vehicles cheaper. As a result, global sales of gas cars have been declining since 2018.
- In 2025, global investments into clean energy are on track to be double the size of investments into fossil fuels for the first time ever ($2.2 trillion vs. $1.1 trillion).

Cities, States, and Countries are Starting to Take More Action

- Greenhouse gas emissions have peaked and are now declining in ~50 countries. The largest emitter, China, may have peaked emissions in 2024 (six years ahead of schedule) due to massive investments in clean energy infrastructure. And annual emissions are expected to finally peak globally within the next few years.
- Cities, states, and countries have passed versions of a Green New Deal over the last five years. These are programs and policies that invest in clean energy, sustainable infrastructure, job creation, and environmental, social, and economic justice. One of the biggest is the European Green Deal, which will likely lead to over $1 trillion in sustainable investments.
- Globally, at least 13,800 cities or local governments representing over 1 billion people have a climate action plan or are working on one. Similarly, 2,350+ jurisdictions around the world representing over 1 billion people have declared a climate emergency.
- Citizens, cities, and states are now bringing thousands of lawsuits against fossil fuel companies and governments around the world to accelerate climate action and make these polluters pay for the damages they knowingly caused.

Business & Finance Are Starting to Wake Up

- By 2025, around 11,000 corporations representing 25% of the global economy had set or committed to setting science-based emission reduction targets.
- Over 1,600 investors and institutions around the world with $40 trillion of assets under management have divested or pledged to divest from fossil fuels.

Everyone Now Knows Big Changes Are Possible

- Covid was hard in many ways, but it proved that society has the capacity to transform *rapidly* if and when we choose to.

The takeaway here isn't that we're on the right track and can be complacent (we're not yet and we can't). The takeaway is that we *are* making progress.

We have momentum and know what we need to do: we need to stop burning fossil fuels and polluting the atmosphere. But to implement climate solutions at the speed and scale needed, we can't just know what we're *against* – we also have to know what we're *for*.

5. Imagining a Better World

The future exists first in imagination, then in will, then in reality.

BARBARA MARX HUBBARD, futurist and author

Mario Andretti is one of the most successful race car drivers of all time, earning the title "Driver of the Century" in 2000. When asked what his #1 tip for success was, he said, "Don't look at the wall. Your car goes where your eyes go."

Good advice for someone going 200 mph while turning a corner. Perhaps just as useful for a society that finds itself speeding out of control.

We've been looking at the wall for decades (or possibly driving with our eyes closed) and are getting closer and closer to crashing into it. To avoid crashing straight into the wall, we need to start looking where we actually want to go so we can make the turn.

In other words, we can't just know what we're *against*. We also have to know what we're *for*.

Now, I'm not saying it's going to be perfect at the finish line – it's not.

Nor am I saying it'll be a smooth ride to get there – it won't be. It'll be incredibly challenging and we'll lose a lot along the way even if we do everything right from now on.

And I'm not saying it will be a fair ride – the effects of global heating are already heartbreakingly unfair and they'll get worse.

What I'm saying is this: civilization doesn't have to crash straight into the wall. Instead, we can make the turn and save and improve billions of lives.

That starts with moving our eyes to where we want to go. It starts with imagining the safer, healthier, and more just world we want to live in.

So, even if you think building this better world is unrealistic (I hear you on that), please let yourself imagine it with me for a few minutes. Because to get from A to B, you need to know what direction to walk in. And even if we only make it part way there, our lives would be *freaking awesome* in many ways compared to today.

So let yourself imagine...

If we moved at lightspeed and succeeded at every turn in rebuilding a safe, healthy, just, and sustainable world where all beings thrive – what would that world look and feel like?

More Vibrant Communities

Imagine your community, after years of hard work, is far more... *beautiful*, inside and out – full of life.

Imagine more trees, flowers, and gardens in, on, and around our buildings and streets – making everything more colorful and calming. Imagine more space in our parks and yards dedicated to native plants and pollinators. Imagine fresh fruits, veggies, and nuts growing in the town square – free food for everyone!

Imagine more people out and about in your community. More bike paths for commuting and recreation. More trails for walking, running, and exploring. More parks and free public spaces for people to connect, play, picnic, and relax. More walking streets and outdoor seating for local cafes and restaurants (plus the mouth-watering scents of food straight out of the oven). More community events, activities, and celebrations. And more local artists and ecological landscapers making all of these places look *beautiful*. This is a community with more smiles, hellos, high-fives, and hugs.

Instead of the noise pollution from gas-powered machines, imagine hearing more laughter, more bird songs, more music, and more moments of peaceful quiet.

Imagine a community where everyone has a safe and resilient home. Where schools have the resources they need to care for and educate students. Where local farmers, artists, and businesses are thriving. Where people know their neighbors and compassion is woven into the fabric of community culture. Where people have each other's backs when times get hard. And where people are civically engaged to ensure the community and its leaders act in alignment with their values and everyone's best interests.

Imagine a world full of communities that are designed for well-being. Where everyone has enough. And everyone is valued.

Healthier Bodies

Imagine a world where every breath you take is fresh. And every sip of water is clean. A world where every bite of food is delicious, organic, and full of life-giving nutrients. A world where *you get extra years of life* simply because your air, water, and food are clean.

Imagine a world where most people walk or bike to work, school, and the store because it's safe, it's cheap, and it *feels good*. It feels good to move our bodies – to get outside for some fresh air, to feel the warmth of the sun, and to be with the people, plants, and animals who make up our community.

This is a world where our bodies are stronger and healthier. We feel better, we live longer, and we have more energy to give to the things we care about most. Not to mention – have you looked in the mirror lately? You, my friend, are definitely looking sexier these days ;)

And it's not because you had the willpower, resources, and awareness to choose the healthy options, it's because society now prioritizes sustainability and the thriving of all life. It's because we designed our systems so that the default options – the easier and cheaper options – are healthier for us and our world.

More Meaningful Work

Imagine an economy that isn't destroying Earth's systems but is restoring and protecting them. It's circular, regenerative, and meets everyone's basic needs. This is what economist Kate Raworth calls "doughnut economics."

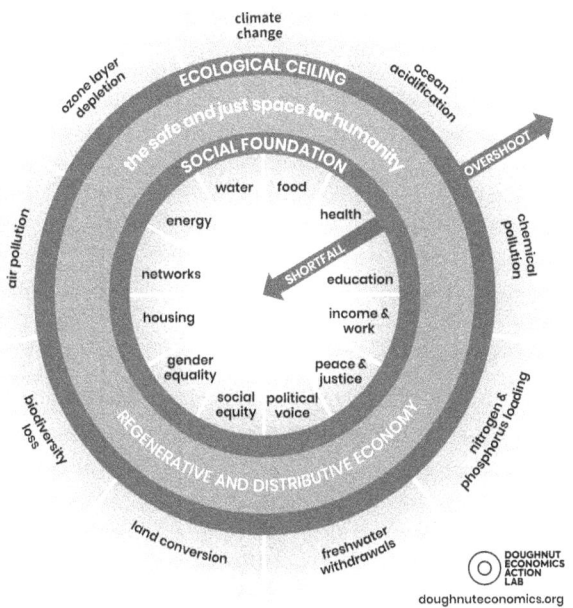

"The Doughnut of social and planetary boundaries." Credit: Kate Raworth and Christian Guthier. Source: Doughnut Economics (2017).

In this economy, businesses, governments, freelancers, caretakers, farmers, creators, artists – *everyone's* work helps meet people's basic needs and protects Earth's systems. Because the planetary emergency taught us we need to prioritize these things – both morally and monetarily – for civilization to persist.

Imagine half of Earth's land and oceans being restored and protected for nature. That means a lot more jobs that need people to get off screens and into the living world. These jobs could be anything from making migration pathways for wildlife to rehabilitating oyster reefs.

No matter what your job is though, imagine coming home at the end of the day knowing that you and your team are making our world better. We spend so much of our lives at work. Imagine it giving you more meaning – more purpose.

Imagine feeling like what you do matters. That you are needed. And that you are a part of something bigger than you.

And imagine working just four days a week (for the same paycheck). We don't live to work or work to live. There's less busyness. Things are more balanced. And we get to reinvest this extra day however we want: by taking care of ourselves, spending time with family and friends, doing things we love, giving back to our communities, resting, etc.

Not only are we more fulfilled because we do genuinely useful work, but we get more time to slow down and live our lives.

Happier Minds

Imagine how much happier you'd be when you and your loved ones are healthier – how much less worry and stress there'd be in a world with less sickness and cancer. This is a reality when our air, water, and food are poison-free.

Imagine a world where society is fairer – where everyone has enough money to live comfortably and support their loved ones.

Imagine a world where things are moving in the right direction – where the future is firmly on track to be better than the past. How much less time would you spend *worrying* about the future? How much more time would you spend *living* in the present? And imagine what this would mean for young people – kids can be kids again without that dark cloud over their future.

Imagine knowing you are safe. That you are a valued member of your community. That your work helps make the world a better place. That you and your family have enough. And that you *are* enough.

Bringing it Together – How Will All of These Things Make Us Feel?

So. Much. Better.

Because all of this adds up to less stress and more smiles. Less sickness and more energy. Less busyness and more time to make memories doing what we love with the people we love.

It adds up to more life. More living. And more love.

Final Thoughts

The purpose of imagining this better world is to instruct decision-making and inspire action today by painting a magnetic picture of how much better our lives will be when we fully implement regenerative solutions.

But I also understand how reading this can feel incomplete, in part because it leaves us with questions.

This vision of a transformed society doesn't tell us how we will overcome the worsening blows from climate and ecological breakdown in the decades ahead. But it does show us how in the overall picture it paints: This is a place that's deeply rooted in connection and care – not only for each other as fellow human beings but for all life on Earth.

Building a culture that better reflects our values of connection and care will be *crucial* to overcoming the significant challenges we will face. To pull through, we'll have to move past today's hyper-individualistic paradigm that prioritizes profit over life and start acting like the interconnected and interdependent beings that we are.

That means prioritizing human rights. It means repairing our broken relationships with each other and the natural world. It means honoring Indigenous peoples' land rights, valuing their ecological wisdom, and supporting their leadership. It means protecting people and the places we can. It means coming together to help each other in hard times. And it means planning for, welcoming, integrating, and supporting the millions of people who will be forced to leave their homes.

It also means true accountability and righting wrongs. The people and companies who knowingly caused this humanitarian disaster must be held accountable. The countries that are most responsible for the problem must fund solutions in vulnerable nations. And the communities most harmed by our extractive economy deserve to be the first to transition to a regenerative one. This is important for keeping the fabric of society strong.

Another natural question you may be wondering after reading this vision…

Is this future world still possible?

I don't know. But I believe there's still a chance if more people step up to accelerate the transformation soon. Even if we can't get 100% of this vision in our lifetimes because of historic emissions, tipping points, or the inertia of our ongoing emissions, maybe we can get 20, 50, or 80% of it. That'd make human systems pretty damn good, compared to today. And *really* amazing, compared to the unthinkable path we're currently headed down.

No matter how bad things get, there will be a best possible future to strive for. And I believe that will always be worth imagining and moving toward.

There are so many other things to say about this better future. Some I already know I'm missing or oversimplifying. And there are surely more that aren't on my radar but are on yours. So I encourage you to build on this vision of a better world. Or imagine your own from the ground up!

There's a better world waiting for us. And we're closer to it than we think is possible. Because momentum is growing and the boundaries of what's possible are changing.

Every step we take and every win we secure makes it more likely for the next one to be bigger and happen faster (even accounting for the inevitable setbacks). Progress toward this better world can happen exponentially.

Let's not forget that rapid transformations in human systems have happened before.

5th Ave, NYC in 1900 **Spot the car**

5th Ave, NYC in 1913 **Spot the horse**

Easter parade in New York City on 5th Avenue in 1900 and 1915. Source: Adapted from Campanale, Carbontracker. 1900: National Archives and Records Administration, Records of the Bureau of Public Roads. 1915: Library of Congress

And that we're far more capable now than we've ever been. So we must remember: the danger is not that we aim too high and fail, but that we aim too low and succeed.

To aim high and move toward this safer, healthier, and more just world, we need to find the courage, love, and determination to keep speaking up and moving forward with others – one step at a time.

Whether you realize it or not, parts of this vision are already happening – seeds of it are growing in pockets around the world today. And behind every success story are people like you and me. Students, engineers, investors, lawyers, public officials, parents, employees, religious groups – people from all walks of life who decided to do something. People who decided to use their power. And in doing so, they are changing the systems they're a part of.

In the next part of this book, we'll explore the surprising amount of power that you have to influence small groups of people – and the surprising amount of power small groups of people have to transform society.

PART 2:
Your Power to Change Systems

6. Small Groups of People Can Change Big Systems

Never doubt that a small group of thoughtful, committed citizens can change the world. Indeed, it's the only thing that ever has.

MARGARET MEAD, anthropologist

We live in a broken system. It's a system where fossil fuel companies get trillions in subsidies while climate disasters intensify. Where profit is valued more than people's well-being and life on Earth. Where our energy, transportation, and food systems have that pesky side effect of *poisoning* us.

It's a system that's so big and complex that changing it can seem *impossible*. But systemic change is not impossible – it's *inevitable*.

The only question is: will *we* change our way of life and laws, or will the laws of nature change them for us?

Will we continue on with the status quo and let our environmental, life-support systems degrade to the point where our social and economic systems collapse? Or will we proactively change our social and economic systems to work within planetary boundaries?

Realistically, it'll be some combination of both. But the more we proactively change our human systems to work within planetary boundaries, and the faster we do it, the better off we'll be.

So, how do we do this?

We Need to Build More *People Power*

The IPCC says we need "rapid and far-reaching transitions" in every aspect of society that are "unprecedented in terms of scale" to stop global heating.

Fortunately, we already have most of the solutions we need to do this.

What we're missing is the power to implement them fast enough.

Dr. Elizabeth Sawin calls this the "power to change direction gap." This is the gap between:

1. Our *current* influence on the decisions that determine future emissions, and
2. The amount of influence we would need to make those decisions climate-positive.

In other words, we need to increase our "power to change direction." We need to increase our influence on the policy and investment decisions that leaders are making at every level. Once we do that, climate solutions will scale up. And emissions will go down.

Other climate experts agree. This is about **power**.

> *"It took me a long time to realize that the scientists had won the argument but were going to lose the fight because it isn't about data and science, it's about power."* BILL MCKIBBEN

The fossil fuel industry has arguably been the most powerful and influential industry in human history. They have invested billions to capture politicians, shape policy, kill pro-climate legislation, influence the reporting of our biggest media institutions, and lie to the public with onslaughts of paid propaganda – all to delay action on climate.

The only way regular people can match the big power and money of the fossil fuel industry is with people power – large numbers of people stepping up, together, to fight for our future.

One last thing on this: it's important to understand that most people running our governments and corporations are not going to do the right thing on their own. And we don't have time to wait for them anymore. *We* have to step up to make them do the right thing. Or replace them with people who will.

Nobody is coming to save us. We need more people to step up so we can save ourselves.

Social Tipping Points

Now, you're probably wondering, "Okay, that sounds great and all. But how many people are we talking about here? How many do we need to actually change the system?"

The answer: not as many as you'd think.

The best way to think about how much people power we need to truly change direction is through research on social tipping points.

A landmark study on regime changes over the last 100 years by Harvard political scientist Erica Chenoweth and their co-author Maria Stephan illuminates something both surprising and encouraging: it only takes 3.5% of a population to (nonviolently) force national governments to change.

When campaigns achieved the active participation of just 3.5% of the population, they succeeded 99% of the time. And many succeeded with far less than 3.5%.

That is a *tiny* percentage of people changing the direction of their *entire country*.

And Chenoweth believes the 3.5% rule likely applies to smaller-scale efforts as well (think: the town you live in, the company you work for, the school you go to, etc.). In other words, you don't need that many people to make significant changes in the places you live and work!

Damon Centola's research, on the other hand, suggests that it takes 25% of a population to achieve *cultural transformation*.

He explains that cultural transformation is complex, requiring the *continuous social reinforcement of new beliefs and behaviors* within our networks of family, friends, and colleagues. However, once these new beliefs and behaviors are adopted by 25% of a population, a tipping point is reached and they spread rapidly to everyone else (think: talking about climate solutions, taking action, caring about the well-being of life on Earth, etc.)

Whatever the true social tipping point is, we are short of it right now.

To achieve transformative change, we need to increase the social reinforcement of sustainable ideas and behaviors. That means talking the talk and walking the walk (frequently!) to build toward that 25% tipping point.

We also need more people stepping up and working together to accelerate action in the places they live and work. We need people everywhere working to make the policy and investment decisions in their spheres of influence science-based and justice-centered. The closer our campaigns in our respective towns and companies are to having 3.5% of the population actively engaged, the more likely they will be to succeed.

To make our systems climate positive, we need more people to come together to change the places they live, work, and belong to.

There ARE enough people who say they'll act. But not enough are taking action yet.

Right now, a whopping 29% of people in the US say they would "definitely" or "probably" join a campaign to convince elected officials to take action on climate if they were asked by someone they like and respect.

But only 1% are currently active in such campaigns.

This is likely a good proxy for systemic action on climate. And it means there are 93 million people in the US who want to take more systemic action but are currently sitting on the sideline, waiting for their names to be called.

It's time to start calling on these wonderful people – our friends, family, and broader networks – to join us.

We don't need everyone. We don't even need a majority of people. So get who's ready to act now and go. This is how we will reach that social tipping point that unleashes the next level of rapid transformation.

And if you're one of the people who simply hasn't been asked to help yet, consider this your official invitation :)

As Dr. Katharine Hayhoe says, "Important problems don't get fixed until enough ordinary people mobilize to take action."

Historical Precedent

We started this chapter with a Margaret Mead quote about the power that small groups of committed people have to change the world. But that quote isn't just inspiring – it's instructive.

Time and time again, relatively small groups of people have succeeded in transforming large, entrenched, unjust systems when most people thought it was impossible to do so.

To kickstart the Indian National Congress's civil disobedience campaign against British rule, Mahatma Gandhi famously led a 24-day Salt March in 1930. The march started with just 78 people but ended with tens of thousands. This action, and many others like it, helped the movement grow to more than 4.5 million members (1.3% of the population) by the late 1930s, and ultimately led to India's independence.

The Suffragettes famously won women the right to vote in the UK and US in the early 1900s. To give you a sense of how big their movement was – an estimated 300,000 people went to the "Women's Sunday" rally in London, while the largest suffrage organization in the US had 2 million members. So even at their peak, less than 2% of people were active in these movements. But they were enough.

Rosa Parks, Martin Luther King Jr., and the Civil Rights Movement led to crucial civil rights legislation being passed in the 1960s. Marches, boycotts, and acts of civil disobedience were instrumental to their success. Based on the membership of key organizations like the NAACP and the number of people at major protests like the March on Washington, an estimated 1-2 million people were active in this movement at its peak, representing less than 1% of the population.

You can also look to Nelson Mandela and the movement that ended apartheid in South Africa or the Gay Rights Movement leading to marriage equality in the US.

Remember, these big systemic changes often feel impossible up until the moment they happen. So don't be discouraged if you can't see all the impacts of your good work or if it feels like we'll never get there. Just keep doing the work. Keep building people power. And *keep going*.

"Never doubt that a small group of thoughtful, committed citizens can change the world. Indeed, it's the only thing that ever has."

MARGARET MEAD

7. You Are FAR More Powerful Than You Think

All that you touch, you change. All that you change, changes you.
OCTAVIA E. BUTLER, *Parable of the Sower*

A key difference between the people who are taking action on climate and the people who aren't is whether they believe their actions matter.

If you ever question the impact of your actions, want to better understand your power, or just want to help others see how powerful they are, this chapter is for you.

Can One Person Really Make a Difference on Climate Change?

I'm sure you've wondered, and rightfully so, how little ol' you, party of one, could possibly make any sort of meaningful difference on the *enormous* problem that is the planetary emergency. After all, you're just one person out of 8 billion people on our planet. So if you're not an elected official or a CEO, you don't have that much influence, right? Does what you do really make any difference?

As shown in Chapter 6, the crucial thing we're missing right now is more people power. This is where you come in. And yes, I know you're just one person – but you absolutely *can* make a difference.

You are far more powerful than you think because:

1. The ripple effect: we are a *highly* social species.
2. You are one of the few people with the power to change the places you live and work.

> "It's time to adjust our lens of how we see ourselves in the world. Our chaotic, intertwined existence reveals a potent, astonishing fact: We control nothing, but influence everything."
> BRIAN KLAAS, *Fluke*

The Ripple Effect: We Are a *Highly* Social Species

Have you ever checked out a new TV show or book because a friend or family member was raving about it? Or tried a new kind of food because someone kept getting it over and over again?

Of course you have – we all have. Behaviors and ideas spread amongst us because we're social beings. Our brains are hardwired to want to fit in with others. When you support certain beliefs, products, lifestyles, or causes, everyone around you unconsciously takes note. You become a point of reference for them. They'll automatically ask themselves if they should do it too – especially if you are close with them.

As Jim Rohn said, "You are the average of the five people you spend the most time with." And it works the other way too – the people you spend time with also take on a part of you. This means that you personally contribute to the makeup of other people – who they are, how they think, and how they act.

Not only does this make intuitive sense, but there is strong research to back up just how much we influence others.

Here are a few quick examples. A study out of MIT followed a network of 1.1 million runners for five years. People ran significantly farther, faster, longer, and burned more calories than they otherwise would have when they saw that their friends ran that day.

Dr. Nicholas Christakis, a Yale social scientist and leading researcher in social networks, conducted a study and found that, "Your happiness depends not just on your choices and actions, but also on the choices and actions of people you don't even know who are one, two and three degrees removed from you."

Lastly, the Asch conformity experiment (worth watching the 4 minutes of live footage online) shows us how powerful social norms are. In each trial, there was only one real subject in a group of several actors. The actors were told to give wrong answers to certain questions to see how the real subject would respond. When presented with incredibly basic, multiple choice questions, subjects went along with the actors, giving wrong answers 37% of the time. And 75% of subjects gave wrong answers at least once. Afterward, they explained that they went along with the wrong answer for one of two reasons:

1. They knew the right answer but answered incorrectly to fit in with the group of actors who were lying.
2. They convinced themselves that their answer must be wrong somehow, despite not knowing why, because the group was unanimous in a different answer.

However, when the subject had a "true partner" (just one other person who deviated from the group and gave the correct answer) they gave the wrong answers just 5% of the time instead of 37%. Having just one partner made it far more okay to act differently from the majority.

This study tells us two things:

1. The behavior of groups is incredibly influential on our own behavior.
2. There is a significant impact when just one person deviates from the norm. It gives others the confidence to follow suit who would've otherwise just gone along with the crowd due to the social pressures of fitting in.

So what does all this mean for climate action?

This is fantastic news! These studies highlight how our beliefs, behaviors, and actions ripple through our social networks. They also show the subtle, but huge impact even one person can have on others in a group.

It means that our actions are far more powerful than we realize. Pretty much everything we do influences people we're close with as well as those we don't even know. So when you speak up about climate change (e.g., how it makes you feel, the risks to your community or business, what solutions are available and their benefits) it makes it more likely that others will too – especially those who would've otherwise stayed quiet to avoid standing out from the crowd.

Solar panels are another good example of this playing out in the real world. When people see that their neighbor has solar on their roof, studies show they are far more likely to get it too, regardless of income or education levels.

When you start talking the talk and walking the walk on climate, others are sure to start following suit. You won't even know all the people you influence. By being the change you wish to see, you will have an outsized impact in helping to bring more people into the climate movement and bring us closer to the positive, social tipping points of 3.5% and 25%.

If you want to see a fun and clear example of this social phenomenon play out in real-time, check out Derek Sivers's TED talk, "How to Start a Movement."

You Are One of the Few People Who Can Change the Places You Live and Work

We need to make every home, town, city, company, school, and institution climate positive.

And the people who have the knowledge, relationships, and credibility to make these places climate positive are, by definition, the people who belong to them.

You are one of the relatively few people who belong to your town, city, company, school, or institution.

So you are one of the few people in the world with the power to change these specific places.

Importantly, you are also what researchers call a "trusted messenger" for the people in these places who you are closest with. Your existing relationships with people and the place you all belong to means you have a much greater chance of reaching and persuading them to take action than others do.

When you combine all of these things…

- The need to make every place climate positive
- You belonging to several of these places that need changing

- Your existing relationships with people who belong there
- Your inherent ability to influence the actions of people around you
- And only needing 3.5% of a given population to make transformative change happen

…it becomes clear that **you have the power to make a difference**.

Every policy and investment decision happening in your spheres of influence is an opportunity to make positive change.

We need to get to the point where the decisions being made in our towns, cities, companies, schools, and institutions not only consider climate mitigation and adaptation but *prioritize* it.

And the beauty of acting on these mid-size systems is that they too have social tendencies.

If your town passes climate policies or makes bold investments, neighboring towns will wonder if they should follow suit (they'll also be able to copy your roadmap). If your company invests heavily in making sustainability a part of its DNA, competitors will take notice and ask whether they need to take action to keep up or leapfrog ahead. The same goes for your school or any other mid-size system you belong to.

Again, you are one of the relatively few people who belong to your town, school, and organization. As a resident, constituent, student, and employee of these places, you are one of the few people who can (and do) influence them.

Implementing the solutions in Chapter 3 and moving toward the vision of a better future in Chapter 5 means changing every school, city, company, and organization. You have the power to do this in the places you belong. And Part 3 will guide you on how to do it.

> *"You are far more powerful than you think you are. Act accordingly."*
>
> SETH GODIN, entrepreneur and author

Whatever you choose to do in your day-to-day life has an outsized impact on humanity's fight against climate change because you influence the people around you and the bigger systems you're a part of.

So here's the hard truth: you can choose to be a part of the solution or do nothing and be a part of the problem. Unfortunately, those are the only two options. You have to pick one or the other because doing nothing is a decision in itself.

> *"What you do makes a difference. You have to decide what kind of a difference you want to make."*
> JANE GOODALL, anthropologist and primatologist

PART 3:
What You Can Do: Top 10 Effective Actions

This is your action playbook. We'll start by helping you find your way – discovering which actions make the most sense for you personally. Then, we'll explore a menu with ten of the most effective climate actions – giving you blueprints to help you level up your positive impact. You don't have to do all of them. But I encourage you to move beyond just the individual footprint actions and focus on changing the bigger systems you're a part of if you aren't already. Ultimately, I hope this helps you find your way, deepen your current efforts, or simply take the next steps that are right for you!

8. Finding Your Place in the Climate Movement

Start where you are. Use what you have. Do what you can.
　　　ARTHUR ASHE, tennis champion and social activist

Now that we better understand the power we have to change systems, let's dive into one of the most common questions people ask: What should I actually *do*? What's the best way for me to plug in? Or take more aligned and effective action?

I think this is where a lot of people get stuck. Which makes sense because the answer to this question is the dreaded, "It depends." Or the more helpful, but still vague answer to start where you are and do what you can with what you have.

Now, I don't have specific answers either. Only you can figure out what the right path is for you.

But I can share some useful ways to think about it and provide questions to help make things easier and accelerate your journey.

I think the best way to start, or re-evaluate if you feel stuck, is by grabbing a pen and paper and filling out Dr. Ayana Elizabeth Johnson's brilliant climate Venn diagram.

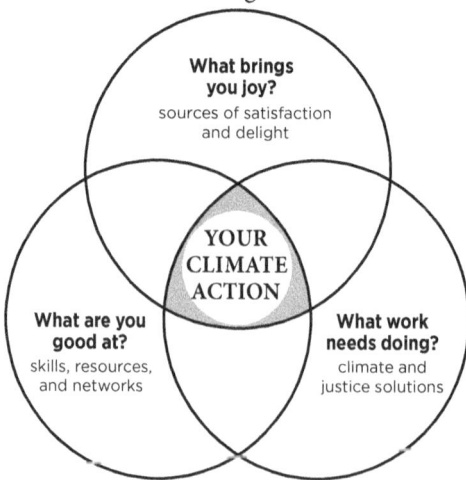

Credit: Dr. Ayana Elizabeth Johnson's *"What If We Get It Right?"*. Used with permission.

> *"The goal is to be in the heart of your Venn diagram, where these three circles overlap, for as many minutes of your life as you can."*
>
> DR. AYANA ELIZABETH JOHNSON, marine biologist, author

This exercise is brilliant because answering these questions helps you discover actions that are in your sweet spot:

- What brings you joy?
- What are you good at?
- What work needs doing?

Let's explore each of these in a bit more detail to help get you started.

What Brings You Joy?

If you're like me, it may help to widen this bucket. So, in addition to joy, you can also think about what you genuinely like doing, what you find satisfying, or what energizes you.

Just write down everything that comes to mind – it doesn't have to be climate-related. For me, it's time with family and friends, playing soccer, helping people, deep conversations, time in nature, learning and connecting dots, an amazing book, laughter, fireflies, and delicious food. Maybe for you it's cooking, dancing, making art, movies, your pet, animals, live music, skiing, traveling, gardening – again, it can be anything!

This is important because we'll be doing this work for a long time and burnout is real.

Part of the reason I ended the nonprofit I started was because, as it grew, more and more of my time was moving away from things I liked doing (e.g., learning, deep conversations with awesome people, writing) and toward things I didn't as much (e.g., fundraising & admin).

So try to make sure that a big enough piece of your climate action involves something you truly enjoy or are energized by :)

> *"Climate touches everything. So stick to what you're good at and what you love."*
>
> DR. ELIZABETH SAWIN

What Are You Good At? And What Do You Have?

These are key questions because we need to leverage our strengths and assets – to use our skills, gifts, and resources to address the huge problems we face. Again, write down anything that comes to mind. And if the voice in your head isn't the nicest (relatable), keep this in mind:

> *"Be gentle with yourself on the 'what are you good at?' question. Set your insecurities aside and consider what you have to offer."*
>
> DR. AYANA ELIZABETH JOHNSON

I wrote: "writing, learning, listening, sports, games, big newsletter." Maybe for you it's cooking, research, technology, accounting, caretaking, leadership, sales, community organizing, public speaking, singing, math, chemistry, languages, investing, entrepreneurship, teaching, or building relationships. Or maybe you have a lot of social capital in your community, a leadership role at work, or a lot of money to invest?

Reversing global heating means bringing all the tools we have to the table. You don't have to know how you'll use them right away, but identify all your assets – anything could turn out to be useful as you let these ideas marinate and begin to connect dots!

What Work Needs Doing?

If you get a little stuck on this, you may appreciate looking at Project Drawdown's list of climate solutions to see what resonates with you. There are close to 100 solutions identified, ranging from solar and coastal wetland restoration to educating girls, refrigeration management, bicycle infrastructure, and net-zero buildings.

In "The Drawdown Review," they also point out that "solutions don't scale themselves," identifying seven "accelerators" that "are critical to moving solutions forward at the scale, speed, and scope required":

1. Shape culture
2. Build power
3. Set goals
4. Alter rules and policy
5. Shift capital
6. Change behavior
7. Improve technology

Keep these accelerators in mind as you think about the work that needs doing!

But, perhaps more importantly, I'd encourage you to think about *your specific spheres of influence.* So take a moment to write down all the things you're a part of: your town or city, your state, your school, the organization you work for, any clubs, teams, or civic groups you're a part of or volunteer at, etc. These are often the places where you have the most relationships, influence, and power to accelerate action. And they all need help becoming climate positive from people like you!

As Dr. Ayana Elizabeth Johnson says in her TED talk, finding your climate action "does not necessarily mean you should quit your job or go start a nonprofit. Quite possibly you are most powerful in your existing roles where you already have specialized knowledge and robust networks. So how might you lean into those talents? Can you help your town, company, church, or school charge ahead with climate solutions? Because what we need is change in every sector and in every community."

You can also ask yourself: Where do these places stand on climate today? Are they taking science-based and justice-centered actions fast enough? Which ones could have the largest positive impact? Where do you, or could you, have the most influence?

For a little perspective, here's a look at the annual greenhouse emissions from some of my spheres of influence.

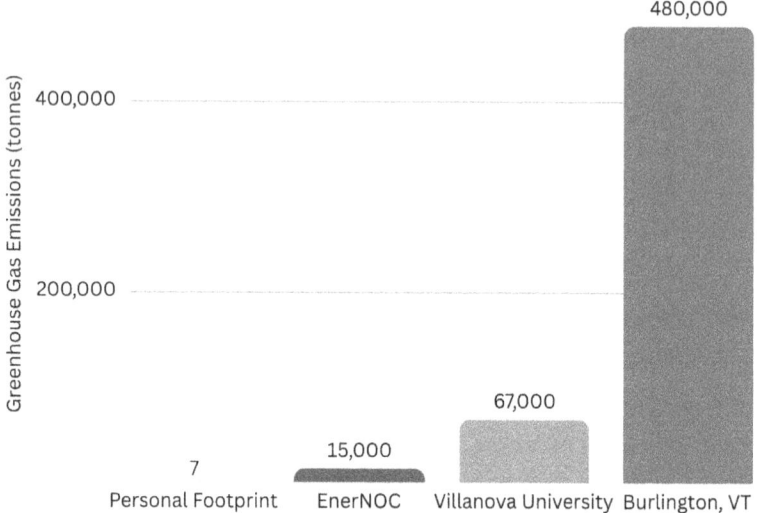

As you can see, my personal footprint is a blip compared to the 1,500-person tech company I worked for, the 6,000-student college I went to, and the 45,000-person city I now live in. Similarly, everything on this chart would be a blip compared to my state's emissions (8 million tonnes) and the emissions of the utility that bought the company I worked for right before I left (70 million tonnes).

I share this to help put everything into context and get you thinking about how big the opportunity for impact is in your various spheres of influence – an important consideration!

Find Your People

Once you've figured out what's at the center of your climate Venn diagram, you need to figure out how to start doing it. Your first step is to try to find other people who are *already* doing it. So ask around and research to see what already exists that you can plug into. Search "climate change" or "sustainability" + your area of interest, town, company, or school online if that's the sphere of influence you want to change. Or search for the specific intersection of things you want to focus on.

Hopefully you'll find an organization that's a great fit and can jump right in. There are *plenty* of awesome organizations doing important work that could use your help, and by joining them you can help scale up their impact.

But sometimes there's a gap. For me personally, what I was envisioning didn't exist yet. And taking the leap to build it is the most impactful thing I've done. What started as a solo project turned into a small nonprofit educating, inspiring, and empowering thousands of people to take more effective climate action.

I'd encourage you to start your own thing if it feels right and is necessary for your given idea, school, company, town, etc. But I honestly hope you can join something that already exists because there are a lot of amazing organizations that need more people power!

Either way, finding your place in the movement means finding your people because working with others is key to getting things done!

Just Take the First Step

I hope you find the climate Venn diagram to be a useful tool (if you haven't done it yet, stop reading and do it!). It can be powerful and clarifying. But if you do this exercise and still feel uncertain about what to do, please know that's normal. Just make sure you don't wait to have every single thing figured out before taking the first step – because you never will. No one ever does. What's important is that you take the first step anyway. And then the next.

There's a great quote about writing that applies to this as well (and life in general):

> "It's like driving at night in the fog. You can only see as far as your headlights, but you can make the whole trip that way."
>
> E. L. DOCTOROW, novelist

Don't let uncertainty stop you from taking the first step. Find the courage to move forward anyway and trust you'll figure it out as you go (you always do).

Lucky for you, the next ten chapters will help make things easier.

My hope is that this chapter helps you decide WHAT to do. And that the next ten chapters help you with HOW to actually do it. Think of them as a menu of effective actions you can take, with each one sharing why it matters and offering a roadmap to help you get started.

- Chapter 9 will help you with the foundational skill of having better climate conversations.
- Chapters 10-14 help you transform the systems you're part of – the places you live, work, or go to school.
- Chapters 15-17 help you minimize your personal footprint and leverage your money.
- Chapter 18 helps you understand the power of activism and how to engage in it wisely.

As you dive into Part 3, remember that we'll start reversing global heating when enough people are taking enough of these actions. We all need to pitch in and do our part, but you don't have to do everything. So feel free to skip to the actions you're most interested in (even if they're a little out of your comfort zone!). Ultimately, the goal is to keep increasing your impact over time in whatever ways feel right for you!

9. Talk About It!

The most important thing you can do to fight climate change: talk about it.

KATHARINE HAYHOE, climate scientist

A few years ago, I had the pleasure of presenting to a class of confirmation students and their parents at a local church. After sharing my story, I started the talk with something like this:

"Now I want to start by asking you a question – what percentage of people in the US talk about global warming occasionally or often with family, friends, or coworkers? What do you think?"

After a brief silence, repeating the question, and bribing them with candy, the guesses started to come in. They were *way* too high (*"75%!, 50, 90, 80"*) until a parent got close.

The answer is 34% (as of 2024). Only 34% of people in the US talk about global warming "occasionally" or "often" with their family, friends, or coworkers. Meanwhile, 66% of people "rarely" or "never" talk about it.

I went on: *"Now let me ask you another question – what percentage of people in the US are worried about global warming?"*

Again, guesses came in all over the place, but this time, they were consistently *lower* than the correct answer. As of 2024, 64% of people are worried about it. So a majority of people are worried about it. But *hardly anyone is talking about it.* Why? What's going on here?

I would argue the decades-long fossil fuel disinformation campaign to delay action and the negligence of mainstream media are two primary drivers of this silence.

But there's also a social theory that I think is worth understanding because it may be at play.

The Spiral of Climate Silence

The term "spiral of silence" was coined by a German political scientist, Elisabeth Noelle-Neumann, during her research into why so many people stayed quiet during Hitler's rise to power.

The basic idea is that people tend to stay silent when they think their view on an issue is different from the majority's (typically for moral and emotionally charged issues). People stay silent because they fear social isolation or losing something, like status, by speaking up.

We're seeing this same phenomenon play out today around climate change. A 2022 US study discovered a huge misperception gap. People assume that only 40% of their fellow citizens support climate policies, when in reality nearly 75% do. Similarly, a global survey of 130,000 people found that 89% of people want more government action, but they assume their peers don't agree.

This misperception that there is a lack of support discourages people from speaking up. According to researchers at Yale and George Mason, more than half of the people who care about climate change "rarely" or "never" talk about it. As Jeremy Deaton, the editor for Yale Environment 360 puts it, "No one talks [about climate change], so no one feels comfortable talking. Silence begets silence begets silence, widening the gap between popular discourse and public opinion, in an ever-descending spiral."

The bottom line is that being concerned about global heating and wanting more climate action is not a minority opinion – it's how *most* people feel.

You're not alone. So don't be afraid to speak up and help break the spiral of climate silence!

How to Talk About it

Wanting to talk about it is one thing. Actually *doing* it is another.

I know it can feel uncomfortable or risky to bring up. Even as someone who is deeply passionate about this, works on it for a living, and inherently brings up the topic every time someone asks me about my work, I feel that discomfort. I "self-silence" more than I should. And I understand why we're hesitant to bring it up.

You don't want to be a downer. You're not sure if the other person cares or not. You don't want to risk getting into an argument with someone.

Maybe you feel like you don't know enough to talk about it. Or maybe you simply aren't sure what to do about it, so bringing it up at all feels pointless.

But this doesn't have to be so hard or scary. And, like anything, the more you do it the easier it gets.

It can also be incredibly beneficial. Sometimes I leave certain conversations feeling more energized and hopeful. Sometimes I feel relieved and less alone. And sometimes I feel much closer to the person, having talked about this important topic in an authentic, constructive way.

Now, it's impossible to give one-size-fits-all advice on this because how you approach a conversation should vary depending on who you're talking to. Are you talking with a stranger or someone you know? Do you know what they think about climate change and solutions or are you unsure? Do you know what matters to them – what they care about and why? Also, what's the context of the interaction? Where are you and how much time do you have? Are you one-on-one or in a group?

These are all useful things to consider. And you should adjust your approach as needed. But, generally speaking, there is a lot of practical advice that can help with *all* of your conversations.

I'm going to break this "How to talk about it" section into two parts to help guide you toward having more, and more "successful," climate conversations. The first part is about your mindset going into the conversation.

Mindset & Strategy for Rewarding Conversations

You want to talk climate with someone. And whether you know where they stand on climate or not, you want it to go well.

Some keys to a good conversation are:

- Respect for the other person
- Deep Listening
- Curiosity
- Being Yourself
- Connecting > "Winning"

These may seem like common sense. But they're easier said than done. And are foundational for any productive conversation.

Let's briefly explore why they're so important, starting with an insightful quote from Climate Outreach's "Talking Climate" handbook on the importance of respect:

> "If the person you are talking to feels respected, valued, and safe, that will build trust – making them more willing to listen to you and to express their own vulnerabilities and concerns. In contrast, fear, guilt, shame, and obligation compromise the quality of the connection between you."

Listening more than you talk and being genuinely curious about the other person's point of view is also key. Put yourself in their shoes. Attune yourself to how they feel. What do they think? Why? What experiences have they had? Learning these things will help you to better understand them as a person and what they care about. With that information, you can find common ground. Listening deeply also means repeating their point of view back to them to ensure you understand it correctly. All of this also has the benefit of demonstrating that you respect and value them (even if you disagree with them).

As always, being yourself also goes a long way. When you're honest about how you feel and why – when you share your hopes and fears

– others are more likely to do the same. Being authentic, imperfect, and vulnerable ultimately shows your humanity. It makes you more relatable and trustworthy.

Perhaps most importantly, your goal is not to win an argument or change someone's mind – your goal is to connect and understand. This is far more productive because when you work to understand someone and where they're coming from, they'll be more likely to try to understand you too. And when they understand why you care, they'll be more open and likely to appreciate or even adopt those beliefs. You won't get this positive outcome if you get into a debate or make someone get defensive. The positive outcome happens over time as a byproduct of conversations built on respect and connection.

Finally, it's helpful to think of each conversation as a mini experiment. Some will go better than others. But you'll learn and get better as you go. Keep in mind that you'll never know all the ripple effects of these exchanges (e.g., how many extra climate conversations or actions the other person then takes, or how they influence those around them). Even if someone gets defensive in the heat of your conversation, they may change their tune later upon further reflection (I know that's happened to me!).

What I'm trying to say is, just speak up – give it a try. And keep trying.

At the end of the day, the best kind of climate conversation is one that happens. Finding the courage to do it is what matters most.

Now, I'm sure you're thinking, "Okay great, this all makes sense. But how the hell do I actually start the convo? Give me specifics!"

Right – let's get into it!

What You Can Say, Specifically

Personally, I like to start with a question. And that question changes depending on the situation.

I find it most interesting to simply ask, "What do you think about climate change these days?" This is direct but gets right to the heart of the matter in a very open-ended way. And by listening and asking follow-ups, you can really understand what they think and why.

But you can also use the (extreme, climate changed) weather as an in. "Wow, this heatwave has been crazy. Global heating is really starting to rev up…" From there you can ask about their health and if they're staying cool. Or ask if their town is investing in resilience (e.g., planting more trees for shade, white/green roofs, water-saving initiatives). Or talk about how it makes you feel and why accelerating action matters to you and your community.

You could also share the latest fun fact you learned: "Did you know that solar and wind are cheaper than fossil fuels 90% of the time now?" Or a not so fun fact: "I just read a Harvard study saying that 350,000 people die prematurely in the US every year from air pollution, including children. Why isn't everyone talking about this? For public health reasons alone, we need to get off fossil fuels asap."

Or bring it up indirectly by asking for advice related to a climate action you're working on. "Do you have any favorite vegetarian or vegan recipes? I'm trying to eat less meat to help with climate change."

You could also share the latest action you took. "We just got a heat pump and love it!" Or invite someone you know to join you for an action. "I'm going to town hall to express my support for more climate action. Will you come with me?"

If you're close enough with someone, you could also simply say, "Hey, do you mind if we talk about climate change? I just really feel like I need to talk about it with someone."

These are just ideas to get the conversation started. The more you ask questions and listen to what *they* think (and why), the better. So if you start by talking about your latest action or fun fact, shift when you can to what they think, how they feel, or what solutions they like.

Some more tips

- If you talk about specific actions you're taking, make sure you're not sending out any guilt, shame, blame, or holier-than-thou vibes because that will make people defensive,

and defensiveness leads to disconnection. Remember, *it's not someone's fault that they were born into a broken system.*
- It's okay to disagree with someone. You can do it respectfully and then try to find common ground. I was recently chatting with a stranger who agreed climate change is happening but thought it was natural and that the consequences were overhyped. I respectfully stated that "We may not agree on this, but I've been working on this for a decade – the data is clear that it is human-caused." He followed up with a question or two and seemed open to believing me. He also seemed open to believing that big oil lied to the public about climate change for decades to maximize profits (I snuck that in when he started talking about Purdue Pharma and the opioid crisis). Anyway, after stating my point, we moved on to clean energy which he was very supportive of. He said the climate conversation would be going a lot better if people talked about it like I did, and not like Al Gore or the Clintons (who he was very wound up about). He even asked me to let him know when this book came out because he wanted to read it! I'm telling you, focusing on respect and connection can open up a lot of doors.
- Some conversations will inevitably turn toward grief or anger. That is fine and normal. Acknowledge and validate the other person's feelings. Feel them with them if it's authentic. But consider redirecting the conversation if it gets stuck in despair. Emphasize the fact that what we do *does* make a difference. And start exploring *what actions you can take* that are win-wins for your life, your family, community, and the planet.
- Finally, as the conversation comes to a close, end with some gratitude. "That was good – I'm glad we talked about that. Thanks."

Meet them where they're at. Connect the dots to what they care about.

Finding common ground around shared values with someone can

be a powerful bonding experience. It's humanizing and helps you understand each other better.

Once you know what someone cares about, you can connect the dots between climate and their existing values. Climate and ecosystems are interconnected with pretty much everything. So you can almost certainly find a way to show how climate change negatively affects what they care about and/or why climate action is good for what they care about. You can show how action is aligned with who they are and what matters to them.

Also, and this is key, you don't need to be an expert on anything to have this conversation. Just be curious about what matters to them. And share how climate affects what *you* care about when it's natural to. Here are some examples to get you thinking:

Are they a parent or grandparent? They, like you, probably care about the future well-being of their kids and grandkids (which is threatened by climate change and improved by climate solutions).

Where do they live? Does their town face increasing flooding, wildfires, drought, sea level rise, water shortages, crop failures, or extreme heat? Talk about what you can both do to make your community safer and more resilient.

Do they love sports or outdoor activities? Maybe they've noticed that the ski season is getting shorter or that there are more days they can't go outside now because of wildfire smoke or extreme heat.

Do they care about public health or the health of our children? They may be interested in reducing air pollution both in the house (e.g., gas stoves) and in the community (more bike lanes, electric buses, and heat pumps).

Do they care about the economy or their community's prosperity? Climate change could cost the world $10 trillion annually by 2050, threatening local businesses everywhere.

Do they like coffee? Chocolate? Wine? Beer? More and more of the plants that give us our favorite things to eat and drink are struggling to survive. Scientists warn some may even go extinct in the coming decades. As the temperature keeps going up, yields will keep going down – increasing prices for our favorite foods.

Do they care about national security? Sports? Traveling? Beaches? Insurance prices? Home values? Fishing? Hunting? Gardening? Cancer? Whatever the person cares about – you can help connect the dots to how climate change impacts that thing. And when the time is right, share solutions and actions they can take to make a difference.

A word to the wise – speaking the language of the person you are talking to goes hand in hand with connecting the dots to what they care about. So put yourself in their shoes. If you're with a progressive, talk about the environmental, racial, and social justice implications of climate change. If you're with a conservative, talk about the themes of personal freedom, energy independence, and job creation that solar empowers. If you're with a politician, talk about how climate policies will get them more votes in the next election. If you're with a business leader, talk about the amazing return on investment climate solutions offer – they not only increase profits but also attract new talent and improve employee retention.

> *"Just about every single person in the world already has the values they need to care about a changing climate. They just haven't connected the dots. And that's what we can do through our conversations with them."*
>
> KATHARINE HAYHOE

Climate change touches everything. So you can find a way to connect it to everything and everyone.

Share your story

Stories are powerful. They may be the best tool we have for connecting, communicating, understanding, and cooperating with one another.

When we listen to stories, our brainwaves and emotions sync up with the person talking. We're literally wired for this type of communication.

That's why I always started my podcast by asking the guest about their climate story. I like to do the same when meeting new people in the climate space. Similarly, when I give talks (or write books apparently), I start by sharing my story with the audience.

This storytelling humanizes us, opens the door for deeper connections and collaborations, and helps bring more people into the movement. It helps build strong relationships. And strong relationships are key to getting hard things done together.

All this to say, knowing how to tell your climate story can be quite useful. So here are some questions that may help you create or fine-tune your story:

- When did you start caring about climate? And why?
- What was your thought process? Did you have any "a-ha" moments along the way?
- What are all the ways climate change and climate solutions impact who you are, where you're from, what you do, and who or what you care about?

Weave these answers into your climate story and conversations. Telling your story of why climate matters to you personally is far more relatable and powerful than any chart, statistic, or the latest scientific study will ever be. As the saying goes, "People don't care how much you know until they know how much you care."

I hope all this is helpful and gives you enough ideas and confidence to have more, and more constructive, climate conversations.

Just please don't let the feeling that you don't know exactly what to say stop you. The words you use matter but it's more about connection and how you make the other person *feel*.

This may be the most important thing to remember:

> *"People will forget what you said, people will forget what you did, but people will never forget how you made them feel."*
> **MAYA ANGELOU**, poet and civil rights activist

This is what all these specific mindsets and tips for talking about climate effectively translate to.

When you truly listen to someone, you make them *feel heard*.

When you reflect back someone's point of view to make sure you have it right, you make them *feel understood*.

When you treat someone like a human who has inherent worth, they *feel respected and valued*.

When you're curious and find common ground by asking what it is that they care about and why, *they feel closer to you*.

All of this leads to more connection. It leads to more trust and openness to hearing your point of view.

This, in turn, leads to more understanding – a stronger relationship. It also makes it much more likely they'll change their mind or behavior at some point. It makes it more likely they'll act on climate in ways that are aligned with who they already are and what they care about.

And it makes it more likely that they will start talking about it more with others – multiplying the impact of every conversation we have.

Why Talking About it Matters

In 2010, journalist Ezra Klein pointed out the obvious when he asked, "Can we solve global warming without talking about global warming?"

Of course we can't.

If no one talks about climate change, people think no one else cares about it. And when people think no one else cares, they are more likely to act like it doesn't matter. This is the self-reinforcing spiral of climate silence.

But when you break that climate silence, the opposite happens. People realize that *you* care about it. That makes them more comfortable and more likely to talk about it too. And the people they talk with are more likely to do the same. There's an ongoing ripple effect.

Every climate win we've had to date started with a conversation. The school district that started composting? Started with a teacher who wove it into a lesson for their students. The town that is electrifying its buildings? Started with neighbors catching up over a coffee. That

CEO who championed the switch to 100% clean electricity? Started with their kid asking what they were doing about climate change at the dinner table.

Of all the actions in the book, talking about climate comes first for a reason – it's a prerequisite for making positive change. It's fundamental – it's step one.

To change larger systems, you need to build power. You need to organize people and build coalitions. You need everyone working toward a common goal. All of this is built on conversations. Conversations to find the people who care. Conversations to analyze the problems and opportunities. And conversations to find common ground, plan, and implement solutions.

Conversations are how we build the relationships needed to get hard things done.

Talking about climate with others is a simple action with an outsized influence. It's the building block upon which all other systemic actions take place.

More Resources

- "Talking Climate" handbook – Climate Outreach
- *Saving Us* by Katharine Hayhoe
- Project Inside Out (For organizations)
- I highly recommend writing a "Dear Tomorrow" letter (link in "Resources & Citations") to someone you love in the year 2050, outlining how you feel and what actions you'll take. This will fine-tune your story and is extremely powerful!

To get more comfortable, you could also join specific climate groups knowing that these people are actively looking to talk about climate change with others, just like you. There are climate cafes, climate beer meetups, climate book clubs, and many climate communities!

10. Help Elect Climate Champions

Don't agonize, organize.
                    FLORYNCE KENNEDY, lawyer and activist

To stop global heating fast enough, we need governments at every level to pass ambitious climate policies. And for that to happen, we need lawmakers who prioritize climate action. In other words, we need more climate champions in positions of power.

But many people, in the US at least, are disillusioned with politics. You hear a lot of:

"What's the point?" Or "My vote doesn't matter." Or "Politicians are corrupt."

I get it. Many politicians have been corrupted by corporate money. They're supposed to be public servants, representing their constituents' best interests, but many of them do not. Not everyone's vote has the same weight. Some communities don't have representation at all in the Senate. And it's far too difficult for simple majorities to get things done due to gerrymandering and antiquated procedures like the filibuster. Overall, the system is not fair, and it's not functioning well. There's a reason experts at the Economist Intelligence Unit downgraded the US from a "full democracy" to a "flawed democracy."

But this isn't a reason to stay on the sidelines – it's a call to get involved and *fix it*. Too many of us think of ourselves as "consumers" when we are, first and foremost, *citizens*. And when I say "citizens" here, I don't mean a legal definition – I mean everyone who lives in a given place.

Civic engagement may sound boring. But it is ultimately about **power**. It's the power to determine what policies and investments are made in the places we live – and who will benefit from them.

Only 71 countries have "full" or "flawed" democracies (45% of the world's population). So for those of us who live in these free and self-governing societies, it's worth remembering that this power to influence and participate in decision-making is a right that wars have been fought over, and people have dedicated their lives to winning for us. It's a right we must cherish, exercise, and protect.

Benjamin Franklin understood this when he walked out of the Constitutional Convention in 1787. Elizabeth Powel asked him, "Well Doctor, what have we got? A republic or a monarch?"

Franklin replied, "A republic, if you can keep it."

Keeping it and, crucially, improving it so that it someday fulfills its stated ideals for everyone requires effort. It requires people to show up and participate in the civic process. There's a reason the first three words in the US Constitution are "We the people."

Too many of us take our ability to influence and participate in decision-making for granted today. We do not use our power. And when we don't use our power, we give it up to others (often corporate interests). As social activist Alice Walker said, "The most common way people give up their power is by thinking they don't have any."

To solve big problems in a dysfunctional system, we need to reclaim and build our power. That means more people stepping up to be active citizens. It means understanding the reality that each of us is part of a much larger whole, that we have the power to improve our community, and that it is our responsibility to do so.

Given the dominant beliefs, norms, culture, and systems (which lead to fairly low civic engagement in the US at least), I think it's helpful to look back in time at an Ancient Roman concept: civitas.

Civitas not only referred to all of the citizens as a cohesive group, but also the laws and culture they created and lived by. It meant who they were *together* – the collective soul of the republic that they were all a part of. As Alex Steffen describes it in "Civitas and the Future":

> "The definition of a civitas ("us") allows an extension of self to include both one's fellow citizens and the public purpose. In that greater sense of self are forged the bonds that allow

people to resist oppression, create public goods, promote equality among citizens, hold accountable their leaders and invest for the future both of today's citizens and tomorrow's. When the ties are severed between citizens, civitas plummets and civic cohesion is lost: public services collapse, public goods are sold off, corruption spreads, disinvestment ensues. People seek limited, blind self-interest. They short the future. They cheat. Being individually weak, and now disconnected, they become easy to oppress (as Machiavelli notes, tyrants don't care if they are hated, so long as their subjects do not love one another). Where civitas erodes away, democracy in any meaningful sense becomes impossible."

Civitas, civic engagement, community – our shared connection and responsibility to the place we live, to each other, and to the future – these have all been devalued and weakened in recent decades. And it shows.

Many of us today take our rights and responsibilities as citizens for granted (in the US, only ~20% of people vote in local elections).

In hyper-individualistic cultures, we don't think of ourselves as part of a larger, interconnected whole often enough. And we don't fully exercise our individual and collective power to shape our future.

But this is all changeable.

It's not that hard for one person to start increasing their civic engagement. And as more of us do it, because we are such a social species, the ripple effect will multiply our efforts exponentially.

This increase in civic engagement is fundamental to making positive changes at the scope and scale we need right now.

With more eyes on the road and hands on the wheel, we, the people, can steer our communities and elected officials with more intention and accountability. We can build places and systems that are safer, healthier, more just, and that work for everyone.

In doing so, we'll also increase our well-being by creating more meaningful relationships with people in our community and being a part of something bigger than ourselves.

The bottom line is this: re-prioritizing community, civitas, and civic engagement is achievable. It's one of the best investments of our time and energy that we can make. It's the foundation for electing climate champions into positions of power. And it all starts with people like you and me.

How to Get Climate Champions into Office

A climate champion is someone who understands what is at stake and will do everything they can to implement climate and ecological solutions quickly, fairly, and safely. We need good, smart, persistent people like this at all levels of government.

Getting climate champions into office comes down to three things:

1. Personally voting for climate champions in every election.
2. Getting as many other people as possible to do the same.
3. Running for office yourself or encouraging someone else to.

Vote for Climate Champions in Every Election

Our climate and ecosystems are the foundation of everything else. And they're falling apart. If we don't take the necessary actions to protect them, restore them, and prepare for the chaos headed our way, all the other important issues we care about are, quite frankly, screwed. So a candidate's climate credentials and plans should serve as a litmus test. If they don't plan on adequately addressing the greatest challenge facing us today, they aren't up to the job. We need leaders who will prioritize this issue, integrate it into all of governmental decision-making, and act boldly – at the speed and scale that science and justice demand.

So, first things first. You need to walk the walk. Make sure you vote in every election from your local school board to the leader of your country. Build the habit. Because it usually doesn't take much time to vote. And when you do, you not only help decide who wins – you help shape the campaigns themselves, the media as it covers the campaigns, *and* the policies that politicians prioritize once they're elected. This all happens because whether you vote or not is public record (in the US, at least). And politicians are incentivized to only care about the priorities of people *who vote*. So when they run for office, and when they make policy and investment decisions as representatives, they are closely following the polling data on what the "likely voters" care about most. If you haven't always been the best at voting, or have forgotten local elections in the past (I just did the other week after moving to a new state…sigh), forgive yourself. And make a plan to vote so it doesn't happen again!

A good plan might include the following:

1. Put all local, state, and federal elections on your calendar so you don't forget!
2. Make sure you're registered to vote. And double-check periodically (vote.org).
3. Decide if you'll vote early, on election day, by mail, etc.
4. Know where your polling place is.
5. Decide how and when you'll get there on election day.
6. Invite your friends to vote with you or celebrate after!

Finally, when it comes to deciding who to vote for, do your research! Who is going to best represent you and your community? Who is the best on climate? Have they signed a "no fossil fuel money pledge"? Who endorsed them and why?

Read the candidate's websites. Watch an interview. And, if you can find a reputable one, look at scorecards to see how strong each candidate is on climate. In the past, I've seen guides and scorecards from: Protect Our Winters, League of Conservation Voters, Sunrise Movement, Grist, Vote Save America, Climate Cabinet, and Greenpeace.

Finally, make sure you know if there will be any ballot questions in the upcoming election. If there are, take a little time to understand the issues so you can vote on them accordingly!

Get a Lot of Other People to Vote for Climate Champions

This piece is crucial! It's how you multiply your impact in elections many times over.

Yes, use social media to encourage people to vote for the best climate candidate. But more importantly, reach out to your friends and family directly. Ask if they plan to vote and know who they're voting for. Share who you like and why (if/when appropriate). And if they live nearby, invite them to join you on election day – turn it into a fun event.

Also, make sure to reach out to your environmentally minded friends because *they're the worst!* Just kidding, they're probably the best, but not when it comes to voting. In the 2014 midterm election, 44% of registered voters voted. Of registered voters who prioritize the environment though, only 21% showed up. Similarly, 10 million environmentalists didn't vote in the 2016 election which Donald Trump won by just 72,000 votes. At the local level, it's not uncommon for races to come down to just a handful of votes, so getting out the vote is crucial.

The environmentalists are out there. But too few are voting. This has to change. And the only way it will is if people like you and me roll up our sleeves and make it happen. So let's channel our inner high-schooler and turn up the peer pressure!

In addition to mobilizing people you know, consider supporting the campaigns and organizations that are getting out the vote for climate champions. You can do that in many different ways:

- Donate to or volunteer with the campaign, or with organizations getting out the vote everywhere (e.g., Environmental Voter Project).
- Write postcards encouraging people to vote.
- Text or phone bank.
- Go knock on doors! Canvassing is one of the most impactful actions because you talk with people face to face.

As with everything, take the actions that make the most sense to you. But don't be afraid to get out of your comfort zone – that's where a lot of the magic happens!

Run for Office Yourself or Encourage Someone Else to

To get a climate champion into office, there needs to be a climate champion *running* for office. But this is rare, even though there is ample opportunity. In the US, most races are won by *whoever files to be a candidate*. That's right – in 2024, 70% of the US's 76,902 elections were *uncontested*.

So, if you know someone who would do a great job, talk to them. Plant the seed and encourage them to run for office. You can also nominate people. Did you know that Alexandria Ocasio-Cortez wouldn't have run for office if her brother didn't nominate her in the Justice Democrats' call for potential progressive candidates?

Better yet – run for office yourself! Perhaps you've never thought about running for office before. But you can do it. Almost anyone can do it – politicians come from just about every background imaginable (also, have you *seen* our politicians today…we both know you'd do a better job than some of them at least). So if there's even a little piece of you that is excited or feels called to this public service, please think about it. Because we need more good, common-sense people making policy and investment decisions at every level of government.

If you choose to run, there are a lot of organizations who would be happy to give you training and support. Here are some in the US that you could reach out to: Run On Climate, Run For Something, Lead Locally, and Climate Cabinet. Even if you just want to chat with someone to explore the idea of what running for office would entail, I'd reach out to one of these organizations to learn more!

I'm guessing there would be *many* people both in and outside of your community who would be grateful for you stepping up in this way to lead on climate (myself included!).

So just keep it in mind.

Getting climate champions into office is absolutely crucial and worth celebrating. But it's not the end of the story. To make our town, city, state, or country climate positive, we need to pass policies and implement solutions. And, as you'll see in Chapter 11, there's a lot we can do to help make that happen!

11. Help Make Your Town or City Climate Positive

They're small enough to get things done, but big enough to matter.

ALEX STEFFEN, planetary futurist

In 2023, people in Cambridge, Massachusetts, celebrated as their Green New Deal became law. It requires large commercial buildings to reach net-zero by 2035, the creation of a green jobs program for low-income residents, and more.

Given that 80% of Cambridge's emissions come from its buildings, this may be the most ambitious local climate policy in the US. And it only happened because people like us worked together for years to bring it to life!

Helping to make your town, city, or county climate positive like this is one of the most effective yet overlooked levers we can pull to accelerate climate action.

Since local government represents the smallest number of people, it's the level where your vote and voice have the most weight. This is especially true in the US, where hardly anyone votes in local elections or shows up to public meetings to exercise their power. So if you do these things, your vote and voice have a disproportionate amount of influence over the policy and investment decisions that shape your community.

Given their size, this is also the level of government that is the most nimble and where things can be done the quickest.

Perhaps most importantly though, you *know* people in your community. It's where a lot of your relationships are – aka it might be the place where you have the most power to organize people and make things happen.

This all adds up to a simple fact: it's easier to get things done at the local level. And that's awesome because the policy and investment decisions made in our towns and cities make a big difference! They can change building codes, zoning laws, the solar permitting process, land use, transportation options, electricity procurement, and so much more.

You may not know the ins and outs of any of these things. And *that's okay* – you don't need to. Just know that your community has a lot of opportunities to act on climate. And as someone who lives there, you have the power to help your community breathe cleaner air and live better lives all around.

If implementing climate solutions in your community sounds like a fantastic, effective, win-win opportunity, it's because *it is*. So let's dive into how you can help make it happen.

What You Can Do to Help

Okay. Let's take it from the top.

The goal is to help make your community climate positive as quickly, safely, and equitably as possible. To do that, you need to influence your local government's policy and investment decisions because they largely determine what will be done and how. And to do *that* you need to build the power to actually influence those decisions.

Building power means getting people in your community aligned on a goal and rowing in the same direction to get there. Since a lot of the work comes down to talking, organizing, and building relationships, anyone who lives in your community and cares about its future can help do this. As Washington state legislator Jessyn Farrell says, "Relationships are the basic currency of changemaking." That's why, as someone who has relationships with other people in your community, there are SO many things you can do to help!

But the most important thing to do is simply to *get started*. Just take the first step.

Getting Started

Like most things, the best action for you to take will depend on your specific city and where it is on its path to becoming more sustainable and resilient.

So the first step is to learn about where your town, city, or state stands on sustainability and climate action. Is your local government doing anything? Is there a climate action plan yet? (If there is, read it!) Any sustainability commissions? Any climate champions in office? Are any local nonprofits or organizations working on the issue? You can get a sense of what is going on by asking around and doing some quick searches online for this info. There may be worthy efforts already underway that you can plug into.

Regardless of where your community stands, what you need to do is more or less the same: help build and exercise the power to influence your policymakers' decision-making around what gets done, how, and how quickly. This is called community organizing.

Keys to Community Organizing for Climate Action

🔑 Find Your People & Get Involved

Talk about climate with your neighbors, friends, and fellow community members. Find out what's already going on in your community and what groups or initiatives you can get involved in (e.g., a local chapter of 350 or the Sierra Club, or your town's sustainability group).

Joining the next meeting is a great way to meet people. Come ready to listen, learn, and share why you care about climate. Once you get up to speed, you can get involved with a variety of different actions – including non-political ones if you're more comfortable with that to start (e.g., helping organize a clean energy fair, a workshop on heat pumps, or volunteering at a repair cafe).

Regardless, the first step is to find your people! And if there isn't an active group, you can start to bring people together. No matter where you live, there are people who care and climate solutions that people can get behind.

🔑 Build Relationships With Your Elected Officials

Do this early and often! While working with a climate action group multiplies your impact, you don't need to build a group before getting started on this. Individual constituents who consistently engage their officials can shift votes, especially on local issues where a handful of voices can tip the balance.

So, whether you're flying solo or with a team, the key is starting these conversations. Get in touch with your elected officials and start building a relationship with them and their staffers. Set up meetings (better yet, try to meet them organically at a community event first before putting on your advocacy hat). Share your story of who you are and why climate matters to you. Ask them what they think about climate change and what they're doing about it. What have they done so far? Do they have a plan for what to do next? Is it strong enough? Are they prioritizing it? If they're a climate champion, coordinate with them and see how you can help. If they're not, you'll have to work to get them onboard. Either way, establishing and (where possible) nurturing this relationship is important for learning about what's happening (if anything), why, and what you can do to accelerate progress.

Corporations pay lobbyists to get meetings with elected officials and build these relationships for a reason: it works!

Keep in mind that legislators are just people. And it's important to meet people where they are. These meetings are an opportunity to better understand them as a person and what obstacles they face. This information is valuable and you can use it to increase your chances of success going forward. Once you understand what they care about, you can connect it to the issue you're working on and find common-ground solutions. Change your messaging depending on who you're talking to and focus on building relationships.

If you're nervous about doing this, just remember that public officials are elected to represent and serve you and your fellow constituents. It is literally their job to listen to you and make decisions in the public interest – and mitigating and adapting to the planetary emergency is certainly in the public interest. If they don't treat you well or don't do what you want them to, you can work to replace them in the next election – and they know this!

So if they aren't doing what needs to be done, make sure you work to get a climate champion into that seat next chance you get (see Chapter 10).

🔑 Show Up & Speak Up at Public Meetings!

Whether it's a town hall, city council meeting, committee meeting, public service commission (they regulate your utility company), or something else, showing up and speaking up at these public events influences decision-making. Share your story of why this matters to you and, as a voting constituent, tell them, specifically, what you want to see happen.

If you don't know what meetings are happening or when, go to your government's website and look at their calendar, or call them to ask. If you're in the US or Canada, you can also sign up for action alerts from Climate Herald, a nonprofit helping thousands of constituents stay up to date with local action opportunities.

Showing up at the various decision-making points in the political process with a specific ask for your elected officials really makes a difference. Your presence and voice can influence the budget, policies, and, ultimately, the direction of your community.

Try to do all of this with other people in your community if you can. Going alone still makes a difference (and you might connect with people there!), but there is strength in numbers, so invite people to join you. I've been on both ends of these invitations – they work, and your civic participation makes a difference (I just had a city councilor flag me down at a bagel shop and excitedly thank me for speaking up the other week!).

🔑 Build a Coalition

Hopefully coalition building around climate action has already begun in your community. But this is an ongoing process either way.

So reach out to environmental groups, local businesses, chambers of commerce, neighborhood groups, nonprofits, and everyone you know to find common ground and build relationships. What do they care about and want to see happen? There is strength in numbers! So connect regularly for an ongoing dialogue about climate action and collectively decide on what your community's priorities and next actions should be. What's the next specific policy or investment that is impactful, enough people can get behind, and is science-based and rooted in justice?

When building these relationships, it's important to get to know who you're talking to and grounding your conversations in what matters most to them. If you're talking to someone who doesn't grasp the threat of the planetary emergency, focus on the climate solutions and co-benefits that resonate with them (health, saving money, etc.). Refer back to Chapter 9 for more tips on having good climate conversations – this is key to everything!

🔑 Step Up – Help Do the Work

Building political will is crucial, but sometimes the biggest barrier isn't opposition – it's a lack of capacity. Many local governments are understaffed and underfunded, so volunteering your time and skills to help them implement solutions can go a long way, even if you're not a sustainability expert. Whether you have experience with leadership, project management, soft skills, or simply have a willingness to learn and roll up your sleeves, there are many ways you can pitch in.

People everywhere are stepping up to do this work for their communities pro bono. Some local governments lean heavily on citizen-led climate action committees to get things done. These groups are often tasked with creating a climate action plan or simply advising and working with the local government on action.

Also, make sure you think outside the box. Sit down and think about all the resources and skills and types of people your community has (look up "community asset mapping" for a useful exercise!). Is there a local college in or near your community? There are likely professors who can help by giving technical guidance or students who are eager to take on projects that will make a real impact. And don't forget about older folks! A local leader I spoke with said senior citizens were his town's "secret weapon" because they have lots of free time, motivation, and resilience.

Finally, and this is crucial, you can help your community get the money needed to make these important investments. This is particularly true if you are skilled at research, grant writing, finance, fundraising, or are well connected. But again, anyone can roll up their sleeves and help by identifying the pools of money that are set aside for investing in local climate solutions. There are often opportunities to apply for funding from the state, federal government, regional planning commissions, utilities, non-governmental organizations, and more. Green bonds are also an increasingly popular option to look into.

Ideally, our local governments would have the capacity to do all of these things. But the reality is that many don't have the time or money to do so. So if you step up and fill in the gaps, you can make a huge difference.

Leveraging Strategic Tools

As your group moves forward, you'll want to have a few powerful tools in your back pocket to help overcome obstacles and accelerate action. Here are a few to consider:

Climate Action Plans
Whether your community has a climate action plan or not, understanding what a good one looks like can help you advocate more effectively. So, first thing's first – what *is* a climate action plan? At its core, a climate action plan is created to answer two questions:
    1. How will your community get to zero emissions?
    2. How will your community prepare for the increasingly extreme impacts of climate and ecological breakdown?

A great plan is made *with* your community. You'll map your town's path from A to B – from where it is now (polluting and unprepared) to where you want to go (climate-positive and resilient).

And the best plans don't just reduce emissions – they multisolve. When advocating, emphasize how climate solutions improve people's lives: electrifying stoves means fewer kids with asthma. Adding bike infrastructure makes our streets safer and brings more customers to local businesses. Electrifying and weatherizing our buildings creates local jobs and reduces energy costs. Nature-based solutions reduce the impacts of extreme weather events and improve our mental health. Like we did in Chapter 5, paint a picture of your community thriving so everyone can see it!

If your town doesn't have a plan yet, you can push for one (along with a dedicated staff and regular progress reports so it doesn't just sit on the shelf). Point to communities like yours that are better off for having one. If a plan already exists, use it as leverage. Quote specific commitments to hold officials accountable: "The plan says 50% emissions reduction by 2030. What's our progress? What are we doing to make sure we hit this?"

Plans can be very useful. But as Climate Planner Adrienne Greve says, the plan is not the finish line – it's the starting line. So you've got to stay at it!

For more detailed guidance, check out organizations like ICLEI and Run on Climate, or Greve's book, Climate Action Planning. And for free local emissions data, check out Crosswalk Labs.

Power Mapping

Power mapping is another useful tool to influence decision-making. It's a way to identify which people and organizations have power – and who might be able to persuade them to take the actions you want.

For example, if your city councilors have a vote coming up for an important climate policy and there's one or two persuadable councilors whose votes will determine whether it passes or not, you could get your advocacy group together and do some power mapping. What are their personal and professional connections? Who in your community cares about this issue and can influence them (e.g., a family member, friend, fellow churchgoer, local business owner, their kid's soccer coach)?

Make a list of these people and organizations who are most with you on the issue and have the most influence with the councilor. These are your strongest allies, and working with them may be key to achieving the outcome you desire.

It is also important to map out the people and organizations who are most opposed to this policy. By mapping out all the power dynamics at play for your desired action, you can see the key decision-makers, the relationships between them, and everyone's level of influence. Once you have this, you'll know exactly where to focus your time and energy to get things done.

Petitions

Petitions are a great way for communities to take matters into their own hands and accelerate action.

They can help in two main ways. First, they let you bypass politicians by getting something on the ballot. This is particularly useful when lawmakers aren't getting the job done – it's a way to give decision-making power to voters directly.

Petitions are also a fantastic way to build up your group of supporters. When gathering signatures for the petition, you can also gather emails and phone numbers. This is huge as you can begin educating more people in the community and invite them to join future meetings and advocacy opportunities!

Citizens' Assemblies

Citizens' assemblies are another effective tactic to accelerate action in a way that is fair and community-led.

Here's how they work: a representative group of people in your community are chosen at random to get together and decide what your community should do about a given issue. Third-party experts are brought in to educate them on the issue, answer their questions, and facilitate the process. It's like jury duty for climate action – and it works!

Why? Because regular people are smart. They learn about the problems and work together to come up with the solutions that work best for everyone in their community.

Citizens' assemblies have become increasingly popular in recent years and can be used at any level of government. Ireland, for example, has utilized citizens' assemblies to not only let people decide what to do about climate change and biodiversity loss, but also polarizing issues like abortion. Likewise, over in London, the borough of Camden turned to a citizens' assembly in 2019 to decide what to do about the climate crisis. Over three sessions, 50 residents came up with 17 climate actions for their community to take. The actions got 75% to 90% support from the citizens' assembly, unanimous support from the council, and directly shaped Camden's climate action plan.

This is about regular people coming together and making well-informed decisions about what their community should do. Unsurprisingly, the public is much more likely to support these decisions because there are no political parties or special interests in the room where they're being made – just their neighbors. Not only does this bypass gridlocked politicians, but it usually leads to bold climate action as well.

So if climate action is stalled in your community, consider pushing your government to sponsor a citizens' assembly. You don't organize it yourself – you advocate for it. Point to successful examples and emphasize how assemblies make your community better. When the people lead, leaders will follow.

Final Thoughts

There's a lot in this chapter. But the most important thing to remember is this: you don't need to be an expert to make a difference – you just need to be someone who lives where you do.

You also don't need to do it all on your own (not even close!). This is a group effort. You just need to find your people and the role that makes the most sense for you.

It won't always be easy. But between making new friends and making your community a better place to live, you may be surprised at how fulfilling this work can be. And how awesome your community can become.

12. Help Make Your Company Climate Positive

> *We don't need to have climate or sustainability in our job titles to be effective agents of change.*
> JAMIE BECK ALEXANDER, former Director of Drawdown Labs

> *The vast majority of the decisions that really matter – that change systems, that reallocate large amounts of resources, that reform policies, that create new plans – all these decisions are made by people whose job it is to make them.*
> ALEX STEFFEN, planetary futurist

Of the 100 richest entities on the planet, 69 are corporations. So it should come as no surprise that companies often exercise more power than governments and citizens today.

In the US, corporations spend 34 times more on lobbying lawmakers than citizen advocacy groups and unions combined. This is likely why there is no correlation between how popular a policy is among citizens and what policies lawmakers actually pass. On its own, this level of political spending is an enormous amount of influence. But it's just one of the many levers of corporate power that we'll explore in this chapter.

All this to say that what our companies choose to do (or not do) about climate really matters. We won't solve the climate and ecological crises unless we turn our corporations around.

Some are *starting* to move in the right direction. But they have a long way to go (e.g., as of 2024, most of the world's largest companies don't have credible plans to get to net-zero, 98% don't have a single board member with deep climate or biodiversity expertise, and they gave nearly 2 times more money to politicians obstructing climate action than to those supporting it in the 2020 election).

The good news is that companies are made up of employees – also known as *people*.

And, it turns out, most people are *pretty* worried about this whole planetary emergency thing that's increasingly threatening everything we know and love. Thankfully, as employees, we have significant influence over the policy and investment decisions that are made at our corporations. Because, as the Director of WorkforClimate, Lucy Piper, puts it, "Corporations don't make decisions – people do."

What Companies Can Do to Become Climate-Positive

One of the easiest ways to tell if a company is truly prioritizing sustainability is if they're focused not just on *"How can we be less bad?"* but also on *"How can we do as much good as possible?"*

This shift shows an understanding that we're in a planetary emergency and that addressing it is a priority for people, the planet, *and* the organization's profits. We are already seeing the climate crisis increase costs and even bankrupting companies in sectors like insurance, food, and tourism, with real estate and others increasingly affected. Former Bank of England Governor Mark Carney warned, "If some companies and industries fail to adjust to this new world, they will fail to exist."

Moving toward true sustainability requires leadership, innovation, continuous improvement, and employees in every department integrating climate action into their roles. It means using the organization's social, political, and financial power to scale climate solutions.

Unfortunately, when it comes to climate action, sometimes it's hard to know if a company is just talking the talk or really walking the walk. One of the most useful resources I have come across to help employees and companies start thinking more holistically about climate action is Project Drawdown's "Drawdown-Aligned Business Framework."

The Drawdown-Aligned Business Framework

As Aiyana Bodi, Manager at Drawdown Labs, explains it, "The framework highlights key areas of leverage that businesses have and associated actions that they should be taking to address the climate crisis. It's about going beyond just "net-zero" and using their influence to level up their climate action, helping not just themselves, but the world address climate change."

This is a comprehensive framework. But don't be overwhelmed by it! Your company isn't going to do all of these things at once. Just think of it as a resource to help you identify and prioritize effective actions. Here is a simplified version of it with six main areas to focus on:

Emissions Reductions

- Eliminate direct and indirect emissions as quickly as possible without relying on offsets
- Set short and long term science-based targets
- Publicly report progress regularly

Stakeholder Engagement and Collaboration

- Engage employees – create pathways for every job to take climate action
- Ensure the board is climate competent
- Help your local community take climate action

Products, Partnerships, and Procurement

- Ensure products and partnerships don't serve bad climate actors
- Require suppliers to adopt science-based emissions reduction targets
- Prioritize circularity and low carbon materials

An eye-opening example comes from Microsoft, which touts itself as a climate leader (and is in some ways). But their specialized AI products for the fossil fuel industry are enabling companies to extract far more fossil fuels now. It's estimated that the amount of additional emissions from these products is many times more than Microsoft's footprint from its operations. Truly sustainable companies wouldn't lend a hand to the expansion of fossil fuels – they'd be working on the opposite.

Investments and Financing

- Offer employees climate-friendly retirement plans and investment opportunities
- Make sure your bank and asset manager are using your money for climate solutions
- Pressure insurance companies to stop underwriting and investing in carbon-intensive projects

If your company uses a big bank, it's likely that 20%–30% of your money is going to fossil fuel companies and carbon-intensive projects. For companies like Google, the emissions from this money can equal the emissions from all of their operations. Check out the "Greening Cash Action Guide" to learn more about switching banks, Carbon Collective or Sphere for climate-friendly 401Ks, and Premiums for the Planet to make your insurance payments a force for good.

Climate Policy Advocacy

- Advocate lawmakers for climate action where your organization operates
- Support mandatory disclosure standards for climate-related risks
- Align political contributions, trade associations, and lobbying dollars with just climate solutions

This is often overlooked but super important. Special interests have delayed meaningful climate policy for decades. That's in part because there's 10 times more money spent lobbying against climate action than for it. To overcome the entrenched power of the fossil fuel industry and its allies, we need other corporations to flex their climate advocacy muscles at every level of government where they operate or have influence. ClimateVoice is a fantastic nonprofit that can help you with this!

Business Model Transformation

- Value long-term thinking over short-term profit and prioritize building a just climate future for all
- Embed a climate lens into decision-making for every part of the business
- Phase out parts of the business that aren't sustainable and scale up those that are

As you can see, being a true climate leader is about much more than getting to "net-zero." It's about maximizing positive impact by using every lever of influence the corporation has – regardless of your organization's size. That means working to embed sustainability into the DNA of your organization and its decision-making processes. If you're a media company, ban fossil fuel ads (propaganda) like The Guardian did. If you're in entertainment or storytelling, weave climate impacts and solutions into more of your narratives like Netflix is doing. If you're an oil company, phase out your oil business and re-invest in clean energy like Ørsted. If you're a small organization, you can use your influence to advocate for local climate solutions (like bike infrastructure that will lead to more customers!).

Being a climate leader means using your company's influence to help make every customer, community, company, and government it touches more sustainable – from lawmakers to partners in your supply chain, the bank you give your money to, and more. Companies have so many levers that can be pulled for climate action – it's long past time *every* department, not just the sustainability team, starts working on climate change.

Now, I know this sounds like a lot (and it is). But you don't have to do all of this overnight, or by yourself. Everyone has a role to play in making your company climate positive – in making it better. And you can help get people moving in the right direction.

What You Can Do

Even with this framework to serve as a north star, you might be nervous to speak up about climate action at work. And, quite frankly, that's 100% valid. Because the truth is that most companies don't want to act as quickly as we need them to (even if they say they do). According to Bill Weihl, the former Director of Sustainability at Facebook and Google, getting companies to change often requires a kind of internal activism – co-workers persistently organizing for climate action. This work isn't quick. And it isn't easy. You'll face setbacks, bureaucracy, and some people aren't going to like it. This action doesn't come without risks, but there is safety and power in numbers. And it's important to realize that you are not alone in caring about this – you're in the majority. According to a recent survey, 83% of employees want to take climate action at work.

So start by finding these people. If there's already a climate action group, join it! If there isn't, think about who might care about sustainability. Make a list. Then start having conversations with them to see if they want your company to take more climate action – and if they want to be a part of making it happen.

Take it one conversation at a time. Chat with one person, then another, and another. The more the merrier, but you only need a few people to start. Once you have a group, set up a meeting, get to know each other better, and learn why everyone cares about this. Then you can begin meeting regularly to accelerate climate action at your company.

To get started, I highly recommend you check out WorkforClimate's "Get Ready, Get Set, Get Organised" playbook or the "Starting a Circle at Work" guide from The All We Can Save Project. These are fantastic resources, and these organizations are happy to help you with this so I encourage you to reach out!

Once people who care about climate change have decided to take action together, the question of course becomes: how can your group help make your company climate positive?

To answer this, I want to share what Jamie Beck Alexander told me when I asked about her theory of change for getting companies to lead on climate:

"To move companies fast enough requires employees – it requires workers across the business to push them faster, hold them accountable, and to find their own ways to contribute."

This two-pronged approach emphasizes the importance of employees tackling the problem both from the top down *and* the bottom up.

Pushing your organization to move faster means getting leadership to throw their weight behind accelerating climate action. Unleashing this top-down momentum is key to getting everyone rowing in the same direction and reallocating resources.

But you don't have to wait for C-suite leaders to come around. As employees, it's important to simultaneously find ways for you and your team to contribute from the bottom up. That means doing what you can do *now* with where you are and what you've got. Just remember:

> *"While every job might not be a climate job, every job can be planet-positive."*
>
> **CHAD FRISCHMANN**, CEO of Regenerative Intelligence

By finding ways to act on climate in your specific role and helping others do the same, you help to build a crucial bottom-up momentum.

When employees work to change the organization from both directions, it makes each one easier – and *both* are necessary to make your company climate positive. Let's start by taking a look at how to push your company's leadership team to move faster.

Getting Leadership to, uh, Lead on Climate

I know influencing leadership may feel like mission impossible. So I want to start by saying that advocating for climate action with your colleagues *does* make a difference – and that you, as employees who aren't beholden to investors or quarterly profits, are the right people to do it. Fifty-nine percent of C-suite leaders say "employee activism" has caused them to increase their sustainability efforts, with even more saying it will soon.

So what does your climate action group need to do to mobilize leadership?

1. See where your company stands. Take a look at your company's climate commitments and sustainability reports and be wary of "greenwashing" (e.g., making it seem like things are far more sustainable than they are). Depending on where your company stands, you may need to push for measuring emissions, committing to climate targets, strengthening the current plan, or aligning the business strategy with the commitments.

2. When the time is right, set up a meeting with whoever is responsible for these targets (often a sustainability team) so you can get connected and learn more. Ask about progress so far, if you're on track to meet your goals, what their priorities are, and how your group can help. Asking how you can help is key because sustainability teams are extremely understaffed (less than 1% of the company) and under-resourced given the scope and scale of their goals.

3. Look at the *"Drawdown-Aligned Business Framework"* shown above with your climate action group and share it with the sustainability team if you have one. Ask: What's our company doing in each of these areas? Where are the gaps? What are our biggest opportunities?

4. Make a list of asks and actions you could take. Many will save money, some won't. Prioritize actions by impact and probability of success (keep in mind there's value to smaller wins early on to build momentum). And consider sending a company-wide survey to demonstrate support for climate solutions (employees note this can strengthen the case for action and lead to big wins).

5. Once you know what actions you want to push for first, do some power mapping. Who are the key decision-makers? How can we influence them to take the actions needed? Who

do they listen to? What do they care about? Who are our potential allies that could help?

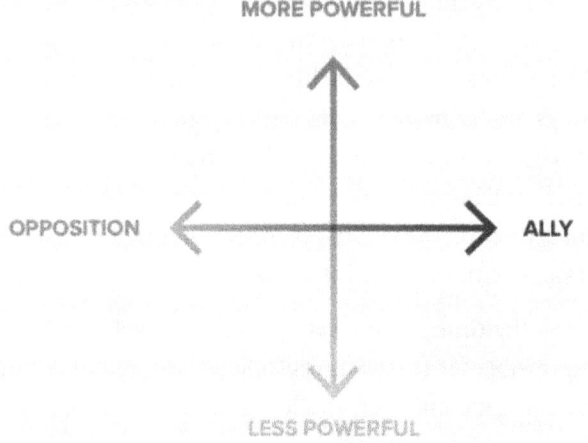

"Power mapping to understand, influence, and identify targets:
Example: getting your employer to publicly support climate legislation

You can use a variety of visual exercises, like this one, to identify the routes to influence decision makers. For example, you may want to get your company's VP of government affairs to publicly support a specific bill related to climate action. While that executive may be hard to access, a power mapping exercise can help you determine a more accessible target that agrees with your ask and can influence the decision maker."

Credit: Project Drawdown, "Climate Solutions at Work"

6. Once you have answered these questions, you can map out your plan of action! When you're ready to present a climate action proposal to a decision maker, ensure that you do your homework, lay out a couple options of how to move forward, and speak in the language of what they care about (e.g., cost savings, increased profits, efficiencies, stakeholder pressure, decreasing regulatory risk, their goals). Show how this will benefit them and the company. And make the decision as easy as possible – so all they have to do is say yes or no.

7. Make sure to celebrate your wins along the way! This is good, hard work – and celebrating progress is crucial for keeping people engaged and building momentum.

Other ideas that can work: writing a joint letter to your CEO, coordinating questions at all-hands meetings, and making specific asks at shareholder meetings. Thousands of employees at companies like Amazon, Immediate Media, McKinsey, and many others are using these tactics to get leaders to act. For any proposal or discussion, it's helpful to show how climate action is a natural expression of your company's core values and mission.

What your group ultimately ends up doing will depend on your company's industry, current commitments, progress, leadership, and culture. But these are the basics and should help get you off to a good start (and starting is the most important thing!).

I want to encourage you again to reach out to the organizations mentioned earlier. They will be happy to help you! Also, the "Drawdown-Aligned Business Framework" is just one part of the "Climate Solutions at Work" guide for employees. And WorkforClimate has some excellent playbooks that will make life easier for your climate action group: "Climate Leadership for Employees," "Emissions," "Energy," and "Money." They also have a 3-month course "for employees motivated to accelerate their company's climate action from the inside" and a community on Slack where people connect and help each other (as does Work on Climate).

One last thing! When talking about your climate action group and your initiatives, remember to tailor it to who you're talking to and to use positive framing. Present the climate action as an opportunity by showing how your company will benefit (e.g., cost savings, high ROI, attracting and retaining talent, customers' growing demand for sustainable products, etc.). So much of this work is about listening to what people care about, finding common ground, and building relationships. Refer back to Chapter 9 for more guidance on this!

Climate Action from the Bottom-Up

While pushing for the C-suite to move faster on climate, it's also important to do what you can without them. There are two main buckets of action here:

1. Integrating climate action into your current role
2. Educating and empowering your colleagues

Integrating Climate Action Into Your Current Role

Whether you're in HR, Finance, Accounting, Engineering, Product Management, Sales, Customer Service, Legal, Government Affairs, Facility Management, Marketing, Manufacturing, Distribution, or pretty much any role you can think of, there are ways you can take action on climate. Again, every job can be planet-positive!

Project Drawdown has collaborated with several organizations to put together an excellent guide for specific roles: the "Job Function Action Guides." These guides help bring the high-level framework down to the level of your specific department and job. I encourage you to do a deeper dive by going straight to the source to find your specific role, but here are a few examples to get you thinking:

If you're in human resources, you can work with your team to give employees a climate-friendly 401(k) option, create more climate-friendly travel and commuting policies, sponsor sustainability workshops, and push for programs that empower employees to take on sustainability projects within working hours. Another big one would be to integrate sustainability metrics and goals into onboarding and performance reviews, and compensation packages (e.g., Apple now incentivizes their executives to hit ESG targets).

If you're in marketing, you can work to end any greenwashing, increase transparency around sustainability efforts, and engage your customers and community around sustainability. You can also help make the business case and push for more sustainable products, as an employee at General Mills did by running media tests to show that regenerative practices boosted sales.

If you're in government relations & public policy, you can work to align your campaign contributions and lobbying efforts with ambitious climate policy at every level of government.

If you're high up in the company, you may be able to make these changes on your own. But, more likely than not, you'll need to work with your team (re-using some of the steps mentioned above) to get approval to implement climate solutions.

Taking climate action in your department is key. But for your company to become climate positive, employees in every department need to be doing it!

Educating and Empowering Your Colleagues

The same climate action group working to mobilize leadership can also mobilize employees across the company to integrate climate action into their respective roles.

This is what Laura Lara Rodriguez and her colleagues at 3M did. Rodriguez is a Project Manager who helped build a highly engaged sustainability community inside the 90,000-person company. That community is now working to integrate sustainability into every aspect of the business! Her advice to you is to "Just start talking about [climate action]. Don't limit yourself with your own biases. You'll be pleasantly surprised by how many people want to do the right thing. Sometimes, people just don't know where to start, and maybe your calling is to help them understand and show them how much power they have."

She and her colleagues took Drawdown's job function action guide and customized it for 3M's business, empowering employees across departments to catalyze action and integrate sustainability into their work.

Similarly, Holly Alpine and Drew Wilkinson helped shift one of the largest companies in the world, Microsoft, by building an internal sustainability community. They weren't on the sustainability team, but they asked for meetings with management, built relationships, and advocated to reduce waste as their first initiative. This work eventually led to Microsoft's first waste-free cafeteria. After that, their sustainability community snowballed to 10,000 employees. As Wilkinson put it, "We changed the paradigm of who got to work on sustainability. Before the existence of the community, the only people that got to work on sustainability were the people that had it in their job title." This employee engagement and power not only led to more employee-led initiatives throughout the business, but to Microsoft making industry-leading climate commitments, launching a $1 billion climate innovation fund, and developing more sustainable products.

Building a sustainability community like Microsoft's takes time, attention, and strategy. To grow your numbers and power, keep talking about it and hosting educational events. To jumpstart honest conversations about how people feel about climate, bring in an expert to facilitate an eco-emotion workshop. To keep people engaged, guide them onto aligned teams (e.g., Education, Steering Committee, Communications) and roles, based on what they care about and what they're good at. To build momentum and credibility, start with achievable projects and work your way up to bigger ones. And remember to have some fun!

Time and again, we see that organizing with your co-workers works. People *want* to act on climate. It just takes a few people like you who are courageous and persistent to get the ball rolling.

As employees, we have far more power than we realize to redirect our organization's social, political, and financial power for climate action – for good. It can be scary to speak up and step up at work, but when we connect and collaborate with others, amazing things can happen. And the impact of these sustainable changes doesn't stop at your company's walls. They have positive ripple effects throughout your community and throughout your sector as competitors take notice and try to keep up.

To stop global heating, every company needs to step up. And that means the employees *in* companies need to step up.

We have to make it happen.

The quickest way to start working on climate is at your current company (and they need your help!). But what if you've tried to make your company climate positive and they won't budge? Or maybe you're ready to leave and want to work on climate full-time? That's great too – we need people doing both! Having an inside and outside game is key to changing the status quo. If you're someone who is ready to leave your current organization (or a student looking for your first job), the next chapter is for you!

13. Get a Climate Job

> *There is no one quick answer to the 'most effective' thing people can do. A lot depends on where people are in their lives. For many though, the most impactful area could be through work.*
> ANDREW WINSTON, author and adviser

I absolutely love it when someone tells me they've made the switch and found a job in climate. Or when they've started a new organization focused on a much-needed solution.

I love hearing this because choosing to work on climate solutions may be the single most impactful thing a person can do. After all, most of us spend more than *80,000 hours* working over the course of our lives. So when you switch to a career in climate, you start investing all of that time and energy into scaling and accelerating the climate solutions our world needs.

But if you've ever tried to get a job in climate, you know how frustrating it can be. So let's dive into some best practices that will help you land a good one!

Identify Your Transferable Skills

If you don't have a background in climate, it's easy to think that you don't have the skills you need to land a job. But, like all of the actions in this book, you do not need to be a sustainability expert to work on climate. There's a good chance you already have relevant skills, knowledge, and experiences that companies working on climate need.

Solar companies, for example, don't just need solar photovoltaic installers (the second fastest growing job in the US, after wind turbine technicians). They also need people with experience in sales, marketing, project management, accounting, finance, human resources, government, public policy – all the standard roles needed to run a company. If you have startup or fundraising experience, there are loads of climate startups and nonprofits that would benefit from having you on the team. Offshore wind companies could benefit from the expertise of engineers, lawyers, or people in the oil industry who have the technical know-how from setting up offshore drilling rigs. Companies working to make things more efficient (e.g., the food system, power grid, supply chains, etc.) need data scientists and coders to analyze and optimize these complex systems. Companies building sustainable infrastructure need people with experience in manufacturing and construction. We also need farmers to make our food system regenerative, electricians to make our buildings climate positive – the list goes on and on!

Also, if you have been in your profession or industry for a while, you know how things currently work, where the problems and opportunities are, and have existing relationships. All of this can be valuable to the new companies working to change the industry and make it sustainable.

The skills and experiences you have can be useful to any number of companies working on climate – just sit down and have a think about it!

For some people, your transferable skills will be enough. But what if you are just starting your career? Or want a specific climate job that requires experience that you don't have? There's often a frustrating catch-22. To get hired, you need to get experience. But to get experience, you need to get hired.

So how do you get climate-specific experience in the first place?

Get Experience

Daniel Hill, the creator of OpenDoorClimate, is an expert when it comes to helping people who want to work in climate. When I asked him about this common conundrum, he told me the top two things people can do to get climate experience are:

> **1. Skills-based volunteering or paid freelance work**: applying

your skills, not just time, to a project focused on climate impact.
2. **Experience-in-place**: finding ways to get experience on a climate-focused project at your current job, either through an employee green group or independently.

Beyond hands-on work, there are now a growing number of 6-12 week courses designed and taught by high-quality organizations where you can learn directly from climate leaders across a wide range of topics. The three best ones that I know of are offered by Regenerative Intelligence, Terra.do, and Climatebase (I was in the Regen Intel one when I first outlined this book). These are great because you learn a lot in a short amount of time, get connected to leaders in the space, learn about job opportunities, and get plugged into a community of thinkers and doers. Which brings us to the importance of relationships (once again!).

Build Relationships & Tell People What You're Looking For

Whether we like it or not, who you know is often a big part of finding your next job. Your connections can give you a leg up by letting you know about job opportunities and putting in a good word for you. But what if you don't know anyone who works in climate? Well, it's probably time to meet some people!

As someone who's introverted and has always had a little social anxiety, the thought of "networking" makes me want to go home and curl up on the couch. But if you told me I could go to something to learn about what climate solutions people are working on, I'd be intrigued. And if you told me I could get to know some of these cool people – that we could nerd out, work on climate solutions together, or maybe become friends – I'd be there. Just think of it as building relationships with people around shared goals and values. You never know what they'll lead to or how you may end up helping each other!

But where do you start? How do you meet people working on climate?

The good news is it's easier than ever to do. You can join Slack communities with thousands of people working on climate that constantly host events and learning opportunities (e.g., Work on Climate, WorkforClimate, My Climate Journey, etc.). You can join groups specifically focused on climate action in your current industry (there's a list for you, categorized by industry in "Resources & Citations"). You can go to *OpenDoorClimate* to find climate professionals who are happy to have a quick chat with you. Or type "your favorite climate solution" + "your skill" on LinkedIn to find people with jobs you're interested in. It's always wise to reach out to people who are already working at companies you'd like to work for, or have job titles that you're interested in. Just send a quick note that explains why you're reaching out, where you are in your journey, and that you'd like to learn from them. Something like:

> *"Hi __, I'm reaching out because I'm exploring a career change to work on climate solutions. I'd love to learn about your experience as a (job title) at (company name) because I believe something like that would be a great fit for me and I'd like to learn more. If you're up for a quick chat to share how you got there and what your experience has been like, please let me know!"*

By having these conversations or informational interviews, you can start building a relationship, better understand what their day-to-day is like, see if that company/role feels like a good fit for you, and figure out what you need to do to get your foot in the door. When you talk, find the balance of asking about their story, what their job is like, and how they like it while also sharing your story, what you're looking for, why, and asking what advice they may have if they were in your shoes. These conversations will help you decide if you actually do want that job, and what you can do to increase your chances of getting it if you do.

Most importantly, just start telling everyone you know what you're looking for and why. You never know who may be able to help or introduce you to someone who can. After much stress and many unanswered applications back in 2013, I got the lead that led to my first climate job in an unexpected place – at my high school alumni soccer game! But it only happened because I was vocal about what I was looking for.

It can feel scary to speak up and put yourself out there – to be vulnerable. But most people want to help. And most people *like* talking about themselves. So reach out to people, be yourself, ask about their stories, tell them what you want to do, ask for advice, and build genuine relationships. When people know what you're looking for, and when you start surrounding yourself with more people in the climate space, your chances of finding and getting that job you want go way up.

Find the Job That's Right for You

In addition to getting experience and building relationships, you can also keep a close eye on climate job boards.

Here's a list of the best climate job boards that I know of. Some will be more helpful than others depending on what industry and role you're looking for. I hope they serve you well!

- Green Jobs Board
- Climatebase
- The Bloom
- Ed's Clean Energy & Sustainability Jobs List
- Queer Outdoor & Environmental Job Board
- Green Job Search
- Nature Tech Jobs
- Terra.do

When you find a job opening you're interested in, make sure you give yourself the best chance of getting it! Look at what the company and its employees are posting about on social media. Do you know any of them? Do your homework on the organization and read the job post carefully so you can craft a cover letter that shows you understand what the company cares about, needs, and why you are the right person for the job.

And if you find one you'd love to do, don't let the job "requirements" stop you from applying! Think of job posts as the company's wish list, *not* a hard requirement.

Any job search can be stressful. And finding a job in climate right now can be especially challenging, sometimes with hundreds of people applying for a single opening. But it's important to keep trying. Every "no" gets you closer to the "yes!" And keep in mind that green jobs are growing extremely fast. In fact, it's expected there will be a shortage of people who can fill the roles in the near future. Although that's not a great sign and points to the need for more climate action education and training, it does mean things should get a little easier for job seekers like you.

Why it's Wise to Work in Climate

When you do land the job, it won't just be good for the climate, it'll also be good for *you*.

You see, sustainability is the future of the economy (and if it isn't, there won't be an economy). We have to get to net-zero emissions globally. And companies will play a major role in making that happen. We will likely be working to mitigate climate and ecological breakdown for decades, and adapting to the impacts for the rest of our lives. So by choosing a career in sustainability, you're entering an industry that is going to be around (more job stability) and growing (more opportunities) for a long time.

But this isn't just a smart choice professionally. It can also be good for you personally. Something clicks into place when your job aligns with your values. It feels good to know that you are making the world a better place – that you are helping save and improve people's lives. You're also more likely to be working with other people who care about solving this. That means you won't feel as alone – that you'll be with people who actually "get it" and are mission-aligned.

So if you're looking for more meaning, connection, and fulfillment from your day job, there's a lot to like about the important work being done in this space. And you will make one heck of a difference by working on climate for tens of thousands of hours.

14. Help Make Your School Climate Positive

There can be no keener revelation of a society's soul than the way in which it treats its children.
                    NELSON MANDELA, President of South Africa

In 2018, 15-year-old Greta Thunberg began skipping school to demand action on climate change. Her question was simple but profound: "Why should I be studying for a future that soon may not exist?"

What started as a one-person school strike snowballed into a movement of millions of students around the world asking their governments and schools the same question. And they're right to be asking it.

Schools exist to prepare young people for their future – to equip them with the knowledge and skills they need to live good lives. But our schools (like most of our institutions) are failing them. They're failing to prepare students for the climate-changed future they're inheriting. They're actively making that future worse by continuing to burn fossil fuels. And, crucially, many are not safe and healthy places for students to learn due to issues like air pollution, lead in drinking water, asbestos, poor temperature control, and being unprepared for extreme weather events. These issues are widespread (e.g., though I grew up in a well-off town, my elementary school was on land contaminated by toxic industrial waste), but they are *especially* bad in BIPOC and low-income communities.

To fix this, we need to make our schools climate-positive and re-orient them to prepare young people and our communities for the realities of the 21st century.

What Climate-Positive Schools Look Like & Why They Matter

To become climate positive, schools need to do two things:

1. Eliminate pollution for student and planetary health
2. Teach students about climate change and climate solutions

In other words, stop harming students. And start preparing them for their climate-changed future. Both are extremely beneficial for the students, the school, the community, and the world. Here's why:

Eliminating Pollution

Eliminating pollution at schools is a no-brainer. When schools burn fossil fuels, they are *harming* their students in the present (air pollution) and future (climate breakdown). But when schools start eliminating pollution, they begin *protecting* students and their future.

For schools, eliminating pollution looks like kids getting to school by bike, walking, carpooling, or in electric school buses. It looks like kids playing on greener playgrounds, learning how to grow food sustainably in gardens, eating more plants and less meat, reducing food waste, composting, and minimizing plastic. It looks like heat pumps keeping kids comfortable no matter how hot or cold it is outside (in properly sealed and insulated classrooms). It looks like kids eating healthy food in the cafeteria, cooked on electric stoves. And clean energy powering everything – let's get some solar panels on that roof!

But the benefits of climate solutions go far beyond stopping global heating. When students breathe clean air and learn in comfortable temperatures, their health, attendance, and grades improve. When schools install solar, batteries, and heat pumps, they become more resilient, giving students and the community a safe place to go during heatwaves, floods, and power outages. When schools embark on all of these sustainability projects, they give students a better education by providing hands-on learning opportunities. And, crucially, when students learn about climate solutions and see them being implemented, it improves their mental health. They see that the problem is being solved, that they have the power to do something about it, and that their community cares about them and their future.

Now, I know what you're thinking: "This sounds great, but how are we going to *pay* for this?"

It's not always easy, but schools around the world are figuring it out. In 2017, the Batesville School District in Arkansas was paying $600,000 every year in energy costs. But an energy audit opened their eyes to a big opportunity to save money. Seeing it was a smart financial investment, Batesville residents passed a $5.4 million bond to cover the upfront costs. The schools installed solar panels, heat pumps, and switched to LED lights. After just three years, these climate solutions helped the schools turn a $250,000 budget deficit into a $1.8 million surplus. They reinvested the money they saved into their teachers who got pay raises of up to $15,000!

Today, most schools opt for an even easier approach to pay for solar – they don't. They let the developer own the system. Schools choose to do this because it means they don't have to pay for the upfront cost of the panels *and* they get to start saving on their energy bills immediately. Whether they own the panels or not, the money schools save by getting solar can then be reinvested in students, teachers, supplies, and more climate solutions!

Saving money and eliminating pollution is crucial. But to truly be climate positive, schools need to not only do less bad – they need to start doing more good. That means looking at all the ways they can make a positive impact *beyond* their footprint. For schools, the most impactful thing they can do is to educate and empower their students to act on climate.

Teaching Climate Change and Climate Solutions

> "Everyone needs to be educated on climate change because climate change and our response to it is going to change the world over the next 25 years as much as the internet did in the last 25 years."
>
> JOE ROMM, physicist, previously at US Department of Energy

Climate and ecological breakdown are rapidly changing our world. But our schools aren't keeping up.

It's past time to stop preparing young people for the way things *used to be*, and start preparing them for the way things are *now* – and for what's coming. Schools need to start (or accelerate) the integration of climate and sustainability education into curriculums – and do it fast.

Students need to understand what's happening, why, and *what they can do about it*. They need to learn about climate solutions (e.g., mitigation, adaptation, and restoration) because that is the work humanity needs to do this century. This knowledge and skillset are not only for self-preservation and protecting life on Earth, but they'll also be increasingly foundational for getting a job. By 2050, we're on track to have twice as many jobs requiring sustainability skills as there are people to fill them. As Melanie Nakagawa, the Chief Sustainability Officer at Microsoft, says, "Addressing the green skills gap is an economic necessity and critical climate strategy."

Since climate and sustainability touch everything, it's not enough to simply add a course or two. These topics need to be integrated into most of the classes offered. This is practical because it reflects reality. Engineers and architects in the 21st century need to understand climate resilience, clean energy technologies, and sustainable building materials. People in finance and accounting need to be fluent in sustainability metrics, climate risks, opportunities, and reporting. Nurses and doctors need to understand that the same pollution causing climate change is also prematurely killing and giving cancer to their patients (8.5% of US emissions come from the healthcare sector). The list goes on and on! We need to understand and work on this problem from every angle and that should be reflected in our classrooms.

While 86% of K-12 teachers believe climate change should be taught, only 42% were including it in their classes in 2019. To close this gap, teachers need more support and training. Thankfully, free resources like Subject to Climate have emerged to help teachers of every subject integrate climate and sustainability education into their classes with curriculum resources and lesson plans (often made by other teachers!). This is a great tool, but it also highlights the need for more systemic curriculum updates like we saw in New Jersey in 2021, integrating climate education into all grades and subjects.

Universities too are starting to make progress. Some of the leaders to learn from right now are Colorado State University, UC San Diego, Dickinson, and Stanford. They have the highest percentages of courses focused on sustainability (22% to 36%) and a high percentage of academic departments offering at least one course on how it intersects with sustainability (85% to 100%). But most schools are far behind where they need to be – and even the ones offering climate education still have work to do.

In 2018, Sage Lenier was a freshman at UC Berkeley. She had been "underwhelmed" by her climate classes that were disempowering and only focused on the problem. So she designed and taught the action-oriented course she had been looking for, "Solutions for a Sustainable & Just Future." Thousands of students have now taken it, with many going on to work on solutions.

As Lenier's story shows, teaching this subject requires great thought and care. Lessons must be age-appropriate and should balance the reality of the problem with solutions that students themselves can enact – especially locally – to give them a sense of agency and power. Crucially, we also need to validate the challenging eco-emotions students feel, and equip them with the tools to navigate them wisely. Teachers may appreciate the "Climate Emotions Toolkit for Educators" for guidance on this!

We need millions more people to implement climate solutions. Given that the purpose of schools is to give students the skills and tools they'll need for their futures, integrating climate and sustainability into curriculums may be the most impactful thing any school can do.

What You Can Do

Whether you're a student, parent, teacher, alum, or just someone in the community who cares, you have the power to help schools make these positive changes. And if you're a student, please don't underestimate your power. You are the most important stakeholder at schools. They exist to serve *you*.

The sections above give you an idea of *what* to push for. But of course, the question is *how* do you bring these changes to life?

Perhaps unsurprisingly, there are a lot of similarities between how to change your school and how to change your company or town. It's all about people power and persistence! The key difference is who the decision-makers are and how to influence them.

Changing K-12 schools and some community colleges is more like changing your town because the key decision makers are members of the school board. They are usually elected by voters, accountable to the community, and tasked with acting in the best interest of the students.

Changing private schools and most universities, on the other hand, is more like changing a corporation because their decision-makers are appointed rather than elected, and less public-facing. University boards are key to eliminating pollution, but for curriculum changes, faculty – especially department heads and senate committees – are likely who you want to work with.

Despite the nuances, the general strategy is the same:

1. **Find your people.** Join a group, or start one by asking around to see who wants your school to act on climate. Meet regularly!

2. **Get oriented. Get clear.** Where does your school stand today? Where do you want to see it go? If you want to change something from A to B, the first step is to understand what those two points are. Once you're clear, write down and prioritize your demands (e.g., increase climate education and get to pollution-free, resilient schools).

3. **Identify and connect with key decision makers** (e.g., your school board). Meet with them. Tell them your story of why

you care about this, and figure out what *they* care about to find common ground for your solutions (see Chapter 9 for more tips).

4. **Advocate for your resolution, policy, or demands.** Keep building your relationship with, and pressuring, the key decision makers. For K-12 schools, show up to every board meeting (with as many people as you can get) and make at least one comment advocating for your resolution or specific demands (find sample resolutions in "Resources & Citations").

5. **Be persistent!** Expect a lot of "no's" and being ignored. Just keep trying to build relationships with decision makers. Keep learning, keep improving your message and approach, keep growing your group of supporters, and keep going. Take it one step at a time. This work isn't quick or easy, but it's worth it. You're guaranteed to learn a lot and you'll probably meet some amazing people along the way!

6. **Celebrate!** Progress may feel slow, but your group will eventually succeed if you stick with it. And key to sticking with it is celebrating all your wins along the way :)

Everyone has a role to play in this! If you're a student, talk to your teachers, your parents, and your classmates about taking action. And organize your classmates to speak up and show up. If you're a parent, talk to faculty, get involved with the PTA, and support your kids! If you're a teacher, start integrating climate solutions into your lessons and use your position to influence the school's decision-makers.

The good news is you don't have to figure it out from scratch. People who have successfully done this work before have created fantastic guides and resources for you!

First, for K-12 schools, check out the "Green New Deal for Schools Campaign Guidebook" by the Sunrise Movement, the "K-12 Climate Action Plan" by This is Planet Ed, or "How to Pass a School

District-Wide Climate Policy Toolkit" by the Denver Public Schools' Students for Climate Action. In the latter, students detail pretty much everything they did, giving you a roadmap you can use all the way down to outreach emails that you can copy and paste. These students talked to a lot of people, met weekly, built relationships with decision makers, showed up at every school board meeting, rallied the support of their community, and, despite setbacks, in just over a year they were able to get a climate policy passed that's making all 207 Denver public schools more sustainable. It's early, but since passing the policy in 2022, the school district has already reduced 8,000 tonnes of CO_2 annually and is saving $5.6 million every year.

The "School Board Member Action Toolkit" from UndauntedK12 is another key resource that you can share with board members to help them get up to speed on these solutions, their benefits, and how to implement them. Similarly, Rewiring America has excellent resources to help you campaign for electrifying everything at school *and* help your school's decision-makers to plan, pay for, and implement these climate solutions.

For universities, take a look at AASHE and their STARS program. They help universities report on their sustainability metrics (including fossil fuel divestment!) so it's a good place to look to better understand where your school stands on sustainability and what areas you should prioritize. Once you've done that, you'll want to dive into the Sunrise Movement's "Green New Deal for Campus Campaign Guidebook" or This is Planet Ed's "Higher Ed Climate Action Plan" for step-by-step guidance.

When you embark on this journey, please reach out and ask these organizations for help. They exist to help people like you and a quick conversation can go a long way!

Finally, I want to share the story of a student named Shiva Rajbhandari from Idaho who ran for his school board as an 18-year-old high school student on a platform that included climate justice… and *won*. He helped get big investments in mental health, a district-wide carbon audit, an EPA grant for electric buses, and stipends to jumpstart green teams at every school. All of this was possible because his presence and relationships helped ensure students' voices and priorities were actually being heard.

Student voices are powerful. As the #1 stakeholder of schools, don't be afraid to step up and try to get a seat at the table for decision-making. Nobody can represent students better than students themselves. And, quite frankly, the more that students get involved, the faster we'll accelerate climate solutions.

Final Thoughts

Most schools aren't prioritizing climate action yet. They aren't fully educating students on climate breakdown. And they aren't equipping students with the tools they need to help solve it.

But many students understand the basics of how bad the climate crisis is and what it might mean for their future. That's why millions have been on school strikes for climate in recent years.

How will schools respond? How will they answer when their students ask: "Why should we be studying for a future that soon may not exist?"

I believe the only defensible, common-sense answer is for schools to become climate positive as quickly as they can and to prepare their students for the climate-changed world they're inheriting. That's how they can demonstrate their worth and give their rightly concerned students a reason to want to go to class.

These things really matter. And doing them will give us all more hope and a better future. But schools won't do this on their own. Change doesn't happen because we want it to. It happens because students, teachers, parents, school boards, alumni, and people like you speak up and step up to make it happen – something we all have the power to do!

15. Minimize Your Carbon Footprint

> *I want you to act as you would in a crisis. I want you to act as if our house is on fire. Because it is.*
> — GRETA THUNBERG, climate activist

Like many people who decide to do something about climate change, my first actions were almost entirely focused on my choices as a consumer and reducing my personal footprint. This is a good instinct. You learn a lot by minimizing your footprint and it's a valuable starting point – just make sure it's not the only action you take!

Why Minimizing Your Footprint Matters

Let's start with the basics. Your carbon footprint is the amount of greenhouse gas emissions caused by your actions each year.

Minimizing your footprint is important for several reasons. First, to be blunt, our carbon footprints cause harm. The pollution we are directly and indirectly responsible for harms people, plants, and animals in the present and future. So reducing our footprint is good because it reduces harm and suffering. Doing this also makes you feel better because your actions become more aligned with your values.

And if you think individual footprints can't be that big, think again. The average person in the US emits ~18 tonnes of greenhouse gases annually (108 pounds/day). For perspective, those 18 tonnes of emissions weigh as much as 9 cars and could fill the Statue of Liberty about three times over. By reducing your footprint, you may prevent tens or hundreds of tonnes of GHGs from entering the atmosphere over time, because our positive impact really does add up throughout our lives. For comparison, the average footprint for people in the EU is 7 tonnes, 11 for China, 3 for Africa, and 6.5 globally. And it's extremely unequal between people. The richest 1% of people in the world (more than $140k income) were responsible for as much pollution as the poorest 66% in 2019. The people who have contributed the least to the problem are also facing the worst impacts, highlighting the extreme injustice of the situation.

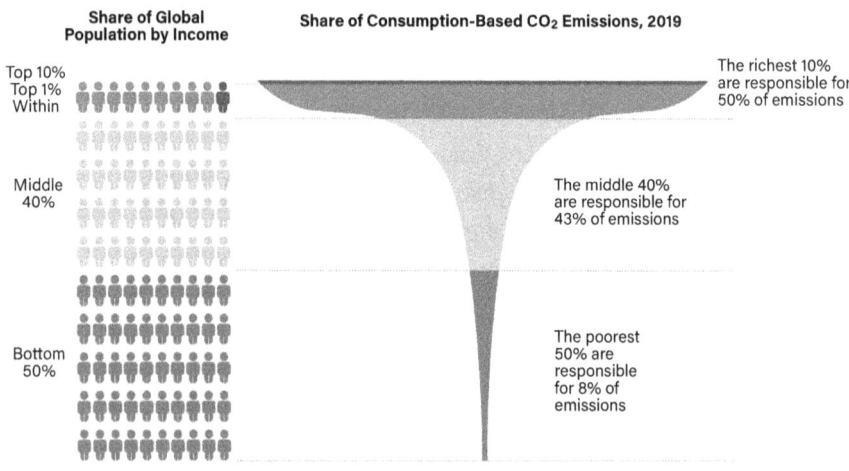

The emissions disparity of the rich and poor. Credit: Oxfam International's Climate Equality Report

The takeaway is clear: people with the ability to minimize their footprint have the responsibility to do so.

Second, reducing your footprint sends a small market signal – a small vote for sustainability. When enough people like you and me make more sustainable choices, we shift the demand. Corporations notice and are more likely to start supplying more sustainable options, like electric vehicles or food grown regeneratively. And when we buy less, less will be produced.

Reducing your footprint also has a social ripple effect. As we talked about in Chapter 7, we are a very social species, and our actions influence the people around us. So when you start making more sustainable decisions, it increases the chances that people around you start doing the same (talking about them also helps!).

Finally, and perhaps most importantly, reducing your footprint helps make you more effective at changing the larger systems you're a part of. This is because you gain firsthand experience learning where emissions come from and how to reduce them. And, crucially, walking the walk in your personal life builds credibility that can help as you organize for larger changes.

My Strategy for Reducing Carbon Footprints

1. **Focus on one thing at a time**

    There are thousands of different actions you could take to reduce your footprint. Rather than getting overwhelmed by all the options (and giving up), set yourself up for success by focusing on one thing at a time. This is a journey. And your positive impact compounds over time.

2. **Prioritize by impact and ease**

    To help decide what to focus on first, ask yourself: What can I do that will significantly reduce my emissions *and* be relatively easy for me? Actions that combine impact and ease should come first because they maximize both emission reductions and the chance you'll succeed. Prioritization will vary from person to person depending on your current footprint, resources (time and money), and personal preferences. For example, if you love hamburgers as much as two-year-old me loved inhaling grapes, then it might be best to start on the transportation or home energy aspect of your carbon footprint rather than your diet because you'll have a higher chance of succeeding. Once you've comfortably integrated the first change into your lifestyle, move on to the next best action for you. Continuing to improve over time is the name of the game!

3. Find the balance that works for you

Nearly everything we do contributes to climate change. This used to really overwhelm me because I don't want to cause harm. And I still have anxiety about the impact of certain actions in my day-to-day life. But I've mostly come to terms with it. We were born into a broken system that makes it practically impossible to get your footprint to zero today. So as long as I'm working to minimize my footprint and maximize my positive impact beyond my footprint, I know I'm doing my best. And that is enough.

At times there's a trade-off between convenience and emissions. Each of us will land at different places on this spectrum for different activities and that's perfectly fine. But I have found many things people assume to be less convenient to actually be quite enjoyable. Walking and biking places or eating vegetarian 99% of the time are things that make me feel good, save me money, improve my health, and align with my values. So give the sustainable actions a try – you may end up liking them better!

Other times trade-offs are harder. I haven't gone to several of my friends' bachelor parties in large part because I don't want to fly anymore (though I usually find a way to make it to the wedding, without flying). I know that a choice like that may sound extreme to some people. And it breaks my heart a little bit when two things that really matter to me are at odds like this. But we're living in a climate emergency, and I'm trying to reflect that reality in my actions while still finding ways to show people I love that I love them.

The bottom line is that I do my best to reduce emissions, improve over time, and let go of my anxiety around them while continuing to live a full life with deep relationships and doing what I love.

Figure out the balance that works for you!

Where to Start & What to Do

To start reducing your footprint effectively, you have to know what it looks like. I highly recommend using a carbon calculator like Earth Hero's (covers 150+ countries) so you can see where your biggest opportunities are to improve. We'll move forward with the average US footprint as an example to give you an idea of what a footprint may look like. Here's the breakdown:

Average US Carbon Footprint (CO_2e)

[Bar chart showing emissions by category:
- Travel: Car Fuel, Air Travel, Car Mfg (~6)
- Home: Electricity, Natural Gas, Construction, Other (~4)
- Goods: Other, Clothing, Furniture (~3)
- Food: Meat, Other, Dairy, Cereals (~2.5)
- Services: Other (~2.5)]

Data source: Berkeley CoolClimate Calculator

Let's take it one category at a time and go over the impactful actions you can take.

Going Places

For the average person in the US, transportation is the biggest part of our footprint. This is dominated by emissions from driving, but for anyone who takes more than one flight per year, flying could easily be the biggest part of your footprint.

Reducing this part of your footprint is pretty straightforward. You can reduce your total distance traveled and/or change how you get to where you're going. So if you can walk, bike, or take public transit to work instead of driving sometimes, that will help. Same goes for when you go to the store or meet up with friends. If you have a car, switch to a more efficient one when you can (e.g., electric vehicles > plug-in hybrids > hybrids > gas/diesel). Also, I understand it's not possible for some people, but see if you can go car-free or get by with a car share program (cheaper than owning).

Reducing total distance traveled is likely most important for those who fly. And that means reflecting on your relationship with flying to see if there are ways to reduce it. For perspective, one seat on a round trip flight from New York to Los Angeles emits ~1.5 tonnes of emissions and melts a cube of ice in the Arctic that's taller than you are (unless you're Shaquille O'Neal). If you're like me and love traveling, consider exploring places nearby and finding ways to do fewer but longer and slower trips.

Again, you'll have to find the balance that works for you. Just keep in mind that choosing the sustainable option usually improves your health, saves you money, and increases your positive impact!

Your Home

This is mostly made up of how you heat and power your house.

I'd encourage you to start by making your home more efficient. A great way to do this is to get a home energy audit (sometimes free) and follow their guidance (e.g., get better insulation, install LED lightbulbs, etc.). I'd also consider moving the thermostat up or down a couple degrees, hang drying your clothes, using cold water for the washing machine, etc. All these things reduce your energy usage and save you money.

The bigger, longer-term project is to electrify everything and switch to carbon-free electricity to power it all. Start by seeing if your town or utility offers a 100% carbon-free electricity option – this can be the easiest switch. It's also worth looking into rooftop or community solar, which saves you more money over time.

Electrifying everything will likely be a series of big investments that happen over several years, so it's important to make a plan.

Here are some tips:

- Make a list of all the machines that burn fossil fuels in your home (e.g., boilers, furnaces, gas stoves, gas dryers).
- Determine what incentives are available to you at the state, local, utility, and federal levels for their electric counterparts.
- Do a little research ahead of time so you're ready to go electric when your fossil fuel machines stop working. They usually break after 10-20 years, so figure out what electric models you'd like to get and make sure your electric panel can handle the extra load.
- Prioritize & plan. Which fossil fuel machines will you replace first? And when will you make the switch?

Bottom Line: Be ready to buy the electric version next time one of your fossil-fueled machines dies, if not earlier! Aka, "When it dies, electrify." *(Rewiring America has a great Electrify Everything in Your Home handbook and a guide for renters as well.)*

Last but not least, if your home has a yard, planting native plants and trees to sequester carbon and support local wildlife is also a wonderful and impactful action.

Altogether, these actions will clean up the air you breathe as well as potentially saving you thousands of dollars over time – a win-win for your family and the climate!

Food

There are two main things to focus on here. First, reduce food waste. Between 30% and 40% of food is wasted in the US. Globally, reducing food waste is a top-five climate solution. And we can all play a part in implementing it.

Second, eat more plants and less meat (bonus points for supporting local, organic, or regenerative farming – or planting your own garden!). Red meat in particular has a massive footprint due largely to methane from cow burps and deforestation to clear land for them and their food. Dairy is also an area to reduce (thankfully, dairy-free ice cream has come a long way!). You can get an idea of the impact of different foods here:

Greenhouse gas emissions per kilogram of food product

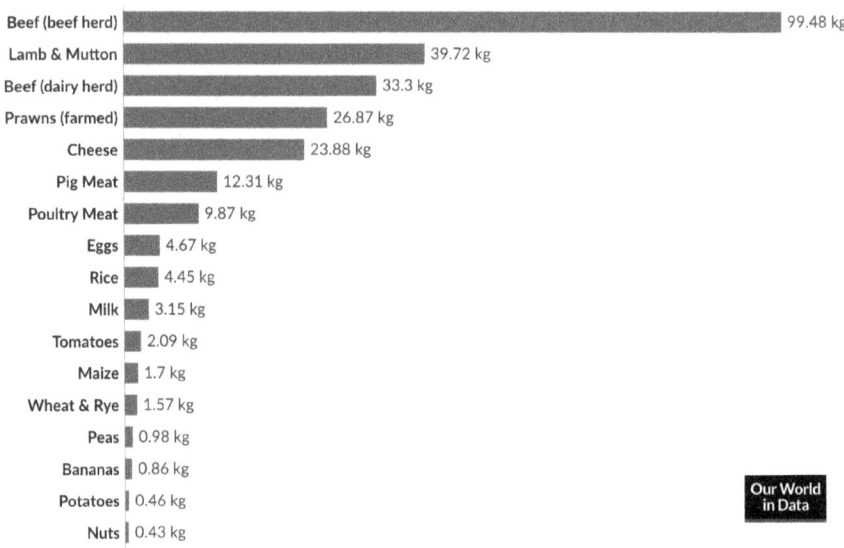

The carbon footprint of different foods. Credit: Our World in Data.
Data: Poore and Nemecek (2018)

A little perspective for people in the US: replacing beef with chicken would reduce your food footprint by about 35%. Going vegetarian would eliminate ~50% of your food footprint. And going vegan would eliminate ~66%.

At the end of the day, this doesn't have to be an all-or-nothing choice. I encourage you to do what you can and start moving in the right direction. I am vegetarian 99% of the time (aka a flexitarian) and typically have chicken or fish once a month while eating out or at someone's house. Largely cutting out meat was easier than I thought (yes, you can figure out ways to get enough protein) and I feel fantastic.

Everyone's dietary needs are different. And you've got to prioritize your health. But keep all of this in mind as you find the balance that works for you. Generally speaking, a diet that is better for the planet is also better for you.

Other Stuff You Buy

Emissions from the goods and services we buy can really add up. So buy less stuff. Don't get something you don't need (unless it's special and is genuinely going to make you or someone you love really happy).

Try to fix things when they break. Get stuff used when you can (clothes, tools, electronics, etc.). Buy local. And invest in higher-quality things that are going to last you a long time.

To summarize:

- Be more mindful of where you go and how you get there
- Reduce your energy usage
- Switch to carbon-free electricity & electrify everything
- Eat more plants and less meat
- Buy less stuff

Taking these actions is important. At the same time, let's make sure we don't lose sight of the bigger picture.

Final Thoughts

It's estimated that 20%–37% of global greenhouse gas emissions could be eliminated by reducing our individual footprints. So it matters and is worth doing.

But also keep in mind that BP spent hundreds of millions to popularize the idea of individual carbon footprints back in the early 2000s for a reason: they want you to blame yourself. They want us to fixate on our footprints because if we only focus on our personal footprints, we're not focusing on systemic changes to get society off fossil fuels.

The thing is, it's impossible for the average person to get our footprint to zero because we live in a broken system. So the next time you feel guilty about driving to work because there's no public transit or bike lanes – the next time you get frustrated that the sustainable option is not the easy or automatic option, turn that guilt and frustration into determination to change the *systems* you're a part of – to make the sustainable option the default option for everyone.

The key question to ask yourself is not "How can I reduce my footprint?" It's "How can I prevent more emissions from entering the atmosphere than I am putting up there?" And the only way to have this net positive impact is by helping to change the bigger systems we're a part of, *in addition* to reducing our personal footprints.

As Dr. Leah Stokes says, "Do not demand that your smallest, personal circle be pure before you start working on the broader circles of community and policy. Because that day will never come. Let's dig in today to shift the system – and tomorrow and the day after. When I come to the end of my life I want the scales to show that I prevented more carbon emissions than I caused. There's no way to make that happen if I work only on myself. My offset plan is activism."

So, like many things in climate, the individual action vs. systemic action debate is really a "yes and." We need both of these highly complementary levels of action!

16. Make Your Money Climate Positive

> *Follow the money.*
> **ALL THE PRESIDENT'S MEN**

What if I told you that the biggest part of your carbon footprint might not be from driving, flying, or powering your home…but from your money?

Many of us work hard to reduce our personal footprint without thinking twice about the impact of our money. But the hard truth is that our cash is not neutral – it's actively funding the climate crisis. When we follow the money, we see that the biggest banks have given *$7.9 trillion* to the fossil fuel industry since the Paris Agreement was signed in 2015. Meanwhile, about 7% of the average US retirement account is invested in fossil fuels. Collectively, these retirement accounts alone make up nearly 20% of the industry's total market value.

But we can change this. Instead of funding climate *collapse*, our money can fund climate *solutions*. And switching is easier than you think.

We're going to break this chapter down into two parts: your bank and your investments. Let's start with what may be the most underappreciated climate action on this list: moving our money to sustainable banks.

How Banks Affect Climate

First, a little perspective. The International Energy Agency made clear in 2021 what researchers and activists had been saying for years: to have any chance of hitting our climate goals, there can't be any more exploration or development of new fossil fuel resources.

And yet, the fossil fuel industry continues to expand – drilling new wells, opening new mines, and building new pipelines.

They can only keep doing this because banks keep giving them money and insurance companies keep giving them coverage. As UN Secretary-General António Guterres put it, "Fossil fuel producers and financiers have humanity by the throat."

It's shocking just *how much* money the biggest banks lend to projects fueling climate change. According to researchers, they lend about 19 out of every 100 dollars to carbon-intensive projects.

It's estimated that for every $1,000 you have in the big US banks, you are indirectly funding 0.24 tonnes of GHG emissions. So the median savings account in the US (which has $8,000 in it) is indirectly funding nearly 2 tonnes of GHG emissions annually. For those with more saved, the negative impact scales up – the average savings account of $62,410 funds 15 tonnes of GHG emissions annually, which is nearly equal to the average person's footprint in the US.

But here's the thing. This is *our* money we're talking about. So we can take it out of the dirty banks and give it to the sustainable ones instead.

What You Can Do

So, first things first, you need to figure out where your current bank stands. Are they financing fossil fuels? Fortunately, Bank.Green and Bank for Good EU have made this easy for us – just type the name of your bank into their tools. *(There are a lot of banks listed, but if yours isn't there, call up your bank and ask them!)*

If you discover that your bank is financing fossil fuels, don't worry – there are some great sustainable banking options now!

Switching to a Climate-Positive Bank or Credit Union

I know switching banks can be a hassle – and that moving your money is a personal decision with a lot to consider to make sure a new bank is right for you. I'll share how I thought about switching banks, but everyone has different needs so I would highly recommend you check out Third Act's "How to Switch to Better Banks & Credit Cards: FAQs" for a more comprehensive overview of factors to consider!

Over the years, I've had my cash with Wells Fargo, Charles Schwab, and Fidelity – I also had a credit card with Chase (yes, the #1 fossil fuel funder). But once I realized what my bank was doing with my money, I knew I had to switch. My top priority was to maximize my money's positive climate impact, so I looked for two things:

- What percent of deposits go to fossil fuels? (should be 0)
- What percent of deposits go to climate solutions? (the higher the better)

I ended up moving my money to Clean Energy Credit Union because 100% of my deposits go to climate solutions. Since they don't have a credit card, I got one from Amalgamated Bank – another top option.

I'd recommend you check out Bank.Green's list of sustainable banks to start your search! You can select the country you live in and they'll share what your best options are.

For those of us who care about climate, it's time to put our money where our mouth is. After switching banks, you'll feel fantastic knowing that your cash supports climate solutions rather than climate collapse!

Switching to Sustainable Investments

Much like our cash, we can also move our investments from fossil fuels to climate solutions.

If you have a 401k or other investments, there's a good chance you own shares in ExxonMobil and other carbon-intensive companies without even knowing it. Owning these stocks has real-world consequences – you technically *own* a small percentage of those companies (and, therefore, are arguably responsible for a share of their emissions). It's estimated that every $1,000 invested in the market has a footprint that's equivalent to roughly 0.086 tonnes of emissions. So, the median retirement account in the US with $87,000 in it has a footprint of 7.5 tonnes each year, while the average account of $334,000 is 29 tonnes.

The good news is that most people *want* to invest sustainably. The bad news is that very few actually do right now because they don't make it easy to!

Not only is this a major values misalignment for most people, it's also financially risky to invest in a dying industry. Plus, it doesn't make a lot of sense for your retirement investments to make the world you'll retire in worse.

As James Regulinski, the Co-Founder of Carbon Collective, points out: we're not going to build the world we want to live in by investing in the status quo or even "less bad" companies. We need to invest in the organizations that are actually doing the most good and building a better future.

Why Moving Your Investments Matters

When you divest your money from fossil fuels and invest in climate solutions, you join a movement of schools, faith-based organizations, pension funds, and millions of individuals that are helping to:

1. Shift the narrative about what is morally acceptable, where the world is headed, and what makes financial sense. (Though hard to measure, this cultural shift has huge ripple effects, influencing everything from startup funding to government policy.)
2. Increase the cost of capital for fossil fuel companies.
3. Decrease the cost of capital for companies leading on climate.

If you don't think divesting can help make a difference, I'd kindly point you to the global divestment campaign that helped end apartheid in South Africa!

Getting Started: Find Out What You're Invested In Now

Normally, this would be a big headache. Mutual funds and ETFs can be made up of hundreds of companies, making it hard to know what's actually in them.

Thankfully, there's a useful tool called Fossil Free Funds that you can use to see what you're invested in and whether those investments align with your values. By typing in the ticker symbols of your funds, not only can you see what percent of it is invested in fossil fuels, but you can also see grades for other important issues you may care about. There are thousands of tickers listed, but if you can't find yours, just keep in mind that Fidelity, Blackrock, Vanguard, and Goldman Sachs invest between 7% and 16% of their clients' money into fossil fuels on average.

Thanks to this tool, it's possible to get clarity on what you own. If you're happy with what you've got, great! If not, here's how to fix it.

Finding Sustainable Investment Options

Quick reminder: I'm a sustainability nerd. And although I studied economics, I am not a financial professional and this is not investment advice. I'm sharing this to educate people on exposure to fossil fuels and the climate impacts of investments. So, as with all financial decisions, please do your own homework and/or talk to a financial advisor!

You may find this surprising, but the hippies over at (checks notes) Morgan Stanley wrote in their "Sustainable Reality" report that, "there is no financial trade-off in the returns of sustainable funds compared to traditional funds, and they demonstrate lower downside risk." So that's the good news you can share with anyone who needs a little nudge.

The bad news is that many "sustainable" or ESG funds are greenwashing (ESG stands for environmental, social, and governance). A recent study found that over 60% of funds with "ESG" in the title had a "D" or "F" rating on at least one ESG criterion. Some of these "ESG" funds hold Exxon for crying out loud!

A great way to find sustainable options is to go back to the Fossil Free Funds tool. You can filter and sort on whatever matters most to you. For example, if I want to find the most climate-positive options, I can take a look at the cross-section of which funds have no fossil fuel companies, no deforestation exposure, high gender equality grades, etc., and sort those by which have the highest percentage of the "Clean200" (the companies making the most clean energy revenue).

It probably comes as no surprise that I personally am a fan of the sustainable investing options made by people who are coming to finance from a climate perspective. One is a diversified climate leadership ETF called ETHO that invests in the most sustainable companies across all sectors, after excluding fossil fuels, plastics, guns, etc. Carbon Collective's ETF, CCSO, and their automated investing services also resonate with me because they only include companies that are working on climate solutions.

Although there's a lot of greenwashing to work through, there are some good options out there! With these tools, some of your own research, and speaking with a financial advisor where applicable, you can find the best value-aligned options for you.

One more thing: if you own stock in a company, you're a shareholder who has the right to vote and influence decision-making. Most individual shareholders don't use this power. But now you can automate this voting through the nonprofit, As You Sow – a simple way to push companies toward sustainability.

Final Thoughts

Zooming out, the world invested a staggering $1.2 trillion in new fossil fuel production and distribution in 2024. But we also invested more than $2 trillion in climate solutions for the first time. We need to get new investments in fossil fuels to zero as soon as possible. And ramp up the investments in climate solutions to an average of $6 trillion per year this decade to avoid the worst impacts of climate change.

So every account we switch and every dollar we move matters. When you make your money climate positive, you are joining millions of people who switched to sustainable banks and a fossil fuel divestment movement representing over $40 trillion.

By aligning our money with our values, we stop accelerating climate collapse and start accelerating climate solutions – we start building, dollar by dollar, the world we want to live in.

17. Donate to Nonprofits Doing Impactful Work

The happiest people are those who do the most for others.
BOOKER T. WASHINGTON, author and advocate

There are SO many important causes to support – human rights, public health, ending poverty, education, issues of racial, social, and economic justice, ending world hunger, animal welfare, and many more. And they're all 100% worth supporting.

But we are at risk of losing all of the gains we've made over the decades in these areas if we don't address the overarching planetary emergency. Because the planetary emergency is not only undermining all of these issues simultaneously – it's also weakening the very building blocks of our society and economy that we rely on for everything: our food, water, clean air, shelter, and livelihoods.

So to continue making progress on all of the important causes we care about, we need to tackle the planetary emergency before it's too late. If we don't start dedicating enough of our time, money, and skills to solving it, it's going to take all the other issues down with it. (Keep in mind that, on the flip side, acting on climate can help improve nearly all these issues!)

Now, given this reality, you'd hope that a significant percentage of charitable donations would be flowing into nonprofits working on the planetary emergency. You'd hope that the smart, passionate, and talented people working on solutions would be getting the financial support they need – not only to do the work but also to be fairly compensated for their valuable contributions.

But climate nonprofits around the world received just $9.3 to $15.8 billion out of the $885 billion that was donated in 2023. That means only 1.5% of charitable donations went to solving what is likely the biggest threat facing humanity today. (To put that in perspective, the world spends $40 billion on Netflix subscriptions.)

We need to change this! Because many of these organizations are doing essential work that corporations and governments won't – they're working to change the system. They're working to educate people, change culture, pass climate policies, transform corporations, win lawsuits, redirect investments, protect land, and so much more. They're working to prevent collapse and build a safer, healthier, and more just world. And they need our help to do it.

What You Can Do

You can support them! When we give donations or volunteer our time, we become partners with the team – helping them to succeed on their mission to change larger systems. At its core, supporting effective climate nonprofits is an opportunity to increase *your* positive impact (in addition to the other actions you're taking).

When choosing which nonprofit(s) you want to support, it's good to do a little reflecting and research. What climate issues and solutions do you care about most? Which actions and theories of change do you believe are most effective? How much of an impact is the organization making? And how will your donation be used?

I know how overwhelming and time-consuming it can be to decide which nonprofits to donate to. So, although there are *many* nonprofits doing amazing work, here are some of my favorite small to medium-sized ones where your time or money can go an especially long way. I've organized them by how they're tackling the problem, so take a look at the categories that speak to you the most!

29 Fantastic Climate Nonprofits to Consider Supporting
To give you a feel for their work, here's how each nonprofit describes its mission in their own words:

Grassroots Activism

Sunrise Movement
The Sunrise Movement is a youth movement fighting to stop climate change and create millions of good jobs in the process. We're building an army of young people to make climate change an urgent priority across America, end the corrupting influence of fossil fuel executives on our politics, and elect leaders who stand up for the health and well-being of all people.

350.org
We're an international movement of ordinary people working to end the age of fossil fuels and build a world of community-led renewable energy for all. Our online campaigns, grassroots organizing, and mass public actions are led from the bottom up by thousands of volunteer organizers in over 188 countries.

Climate Changemakers
Climate Changemakers is a modern climate advocacy network built for busy, productive people who are looking for meaningful civic engagement. We advance systems-level climate solutions through strategic advocacy.

Extinction Rebellion
Extinction Rebellion is a decentralised, international and politically non-partisan movement using non-violent direct action and civil disobedience to persuade governments to act justly on the Climate and Ecological Emergency.

The All We Can Save Project
We believe people are the heart of planetary healing. Building on our founding anthology, *All We Can Save*, our work supports thousands of climate doers, thinkers, and feelers. Climate Wayfinding, our flagship program, helps people move toward clarity, courage, connection, and contribution on their climate journeys. It's taking root at universities across the U.S. and Canada—and beyond.

Third Act
Third Act is the only nationwide effort to mobilize older Americans

into campaigns that safeguard democracy and protect our climate. With 70+ million people, these reliable voters/consumers can heavily influence Wall Street and Washington. We leverage their strengths: fewer time constraints, decades of skill building, and a sense of purpose in fighting to preserve a safe and livable world for future generations.

Climate Emergency Fund
We support climate activists who use disruptive tactics – interrupting politicians' speeches, occupying fossil fuel infrastructure, and more – because these approaches grab the media's and public's attention and raise the alarm about the climate emergency. While controversial, these tactics are backed by social science and history. Climate activists are passionate, brave volunteers who are trying to protect all of us. They are woefully underfunded and deserve our support.

Global Greengrants Fund
Since 1993, Global Greengrants Fund has been one of the leading organizations in the world supporting grassroots-led efforts to protect the planet and the rights of people. How do we do it? We let local people take the lead…we trust local people to advance solutions and strategies that will best fit their needs, providing them the resources to make their ideas a reality.

Environmental Justice & Frontline Communities

WE ACT for Environmental Justice
Founded in 1988, WE ACT for Environmental Justice is a community-based organization headquartered in Harlem. We strive to build healthy communities and ensure that people of color and low-income participate in and benefit from the creation of equitable environmental policies and programs at the City, State, and Federal levels.

Taproot Earth
Taproot seeds global campaigns and self-governing Formations that address the root cause of the climate crisis, reimagine sustainable solutions, and shift structures necessary to create a more sustainable world. Our solutions to the climate crisis go far beyond carbon

reduction and greenhouse gas mitigation. They are rooted in community stewardship and governance of water, energy, and land.

Rainforest Foundation US

Since their founding, Rainforest Foundation US has supported securing over 43 million acres of Indigenous peoples' land through titling and demarcation, and helped develop a proven, grassroots approach to preventing deforestation on Indigenous peoples' lands for as little as $2 per acre per year.

Indigenous Environmental Network

IEN was formed by grassroots Indigenous peoples and individuals to address environmental and economic justice issues. IEN's activities include building the capacity of Indigenous communities and tribal governments to develop mechanisms to protect our sacred sites, land, water, air, natural resources, health of both our people and all living things, and to build economically sustainable communities.

Honor the Earth

Honor the Earth is committed to protecting the lifeways and sovereignty of our Indigenous Relatives across Mother Earth. We do this by investing in our communities and a new generation of organizers through campaigns, research, training, reclaiming our narrative, and providing capacity support in service of all land and life.

The Deep South Center for Environmental Justice

The Deep South Center for Environmental Justice is dedicated to improving the lives of community members of all ages who are harmed by pollution and vulnerable to climate change through research and policy studies, community and student engagement to impact policy change, and health and safety training for environmental careers.

Intersectional Environmentalist

Intersectional Environmentalist is an eco-media company deepening environmental awareness and inspiring climate action through the power of art, education, and storytelling. We envision a world where storytelling unites communities to foster climate action and collective resilience, and create resources and programs that connect all people to the climate justice movement.

US Electoral & Political Advocacy

Environmental Voter Project
We identify inactive environmentalists and transform them into consistent voters to build the power of the environmental movement.

Run On Climate
Run On Climate works to pass cutting-edge climate policies in cities across the U.S. by electing climate champions into local offices and collaborating with elected officials and advocates. Your donation (or volunteering!) can help us flip critical local races and enact the strongest climate policies in U.S. history, helping cities and towns in the race to zero pollution.

Climate Solutions

Global Solutions Alliance
The Global Solutions Alliance (GSA) unites individuals and organizations to drive collective impact through holistic, science-based tools. By empowering policymakers, investors, NGOs, and decision-makers, GSA accelerates climate solutions, advances global sustainability goals, and builds regenerative economies and societies in harmony with nature.

Multisolving Institute
Multisolving is an innovative approach to tackling climate, health, and equity challenges with one investment of time or resources. Multisolving Institute supports this work by providing research, tools, and stories to help people design solutions that accelerate multisolving across sectors.

Climate Curve
Climate Curve gives away over half a million in prizes yearly to decarbonize the planet and resources the 2000+ vetted organizations in our Climate Impact Conduit community with talent through placing 500+ Constellations Fellows and enabling winners to raise 10x the prize amount in additional capital.

Public Policy & Research

Rewiring America
Rewiring America is the leading electrification nonprofit focused on electrifying our homes, communities, and businesses. We develop accessible data and tools and build coalitions and partnerships to make going electric easier for households and communities. We help Americans save money, tackle nationwide emissions goals, improve health, and build the next generation of the clean energy workforce.

Evergreen Action
Evergreen is leading the fight to put bold climate action at the top of America's agenda, implement an all-out mobilization to defeat climate change and create millions of jobs in a clean energy economy. We empower climate and community leaders, and advocate for policymakers to adopt the urgent climate policies that science demands.

Journalism

Grist
Grist is a nonprofit, independent media organization dedicated to reporting on climate change. We seek to document the often unequal impacts of climate change on communities in the United States and globally — as well as to show the promise of equitable climate solutions.

Inside Climate News
Founded in 2007, Inside Climate News is a Pulitzer Prize-winning, nonprofit, nonpartisan news organization that provides essential reporting and analysis on climate change, energy and the environment, for the public and for decision makers. We serve as watchdogs of government, industry, and advocacy groups and hold them accountable for their policies and actions.

Corporate Action

ClimateVoice
Our mission is to mobilize the voice of the workforce to urge

companies to go "all in" on climate, both in business practices and policy advocacy.

WorkforClimate
At WorkforClimate, we're building a movement of employees inside corporations, committed to bold, organised climate action—not business as usual. We're a non-profit (NGO) advocating for climate policy that drives corporate climate action. And we do that by helping employees from across the corporate sector to become effective climate leaders at work.

Girls' Education and Women's Leadership

CAMFED
CAMFED is a pan-African organization combating poverty, inequality, injustice, and the climate crisis through girls' education and women's leadership.

Law

ClientEarth
We use the power of law to bring about systemic change that protects the earth for – and with – its inhabitants.

Earthjustice
Earthjustice is the nation's leading environmental law organization. Our attorneys fight for everyone's right to a healthy environment free of charge, because we believe the earth needs a good lawyer.

Final Thoughts

Once you've decided which organizations to support, make sure your giving is as impactful as possible.

That means giving consistently. While one-time donations are fantastic, recurring donations are especially helpful for nonprofits because they enable them to plan for the future, reduce fundraising costs, and focus on their mission.

When it comes to deciding how much to donate, consider giving a percentage of your annual salary. Whether it's 10%, 5%, 1%, or something else, it's the commitment to pitching in that matters. Giving a percentage may sound daunting, but the 67% of people in the US who donate typically give 2% of their income on average. For someone with a median income of $42,000, that's about $70/month.

The bottom line is to give what you can, and do it consistently. If money is tight, start small. Even if you're only able to give a few dollars a month, that helps! As do any other ways you can support (e.g., volunteering your time, skills, or helping to spread the word about their work!).

Giving our time and money to mission-driven nonprofits isn't just charity – it's an investment in our future. It's an opportunity to scale up our positive impact and join forces with others to build a better world. And, quite frankly, it's a chance to feel great about doing your part.

18. Peacefully Protesting & Civil Resistance

Power concedes nothing without a demand. It never did and it never will.

FREDERICK DOUGLASS, abolitionist and author

In April 2019, Extinction Rebellion brought London to a standstill. For eleven days straight, thousands of people – kids, parents, grandparents – sat down on bridges and refused to move. Combined with the ongoing efforts of students striking with Fridays for Future, the UK government felt the heat. Within weeks they declared a climate emergency and passed a net-zero by 2050 target into law.

This is the power of peacefully protesting and civil resistance. And we need a lot more of it!

Up to this point, all the actions we've covered work to change the system *internally* – playing by the established rules of how to go about changing things. To be clear, these actions are important, need to be done, and can move the needle when enough people do them. But, quite frankly, those actions *alone* won't get climate solutions implemented fast enough. People have been trying to change the system from the inside for decades while emissions have only gone in one direction: up.

So the climate movement needs more people going beyond just the "proper" avenues of change. To get off fossil fuels and reverse global heating fast enough, we need way more people pushing from *the outside* for transformational climate action.

In other words, we need more activists. We need more people in the streets, joining civil resistance campaigns (think: peaceful protests, strikes, boycotts, sit-ins, etc.) that disrupt the status quo and change the conventional wisdom of what is possible – of how quickly we should be implementing climate solutions.

As someone who grew up with social anxiety, is conflict-averse, and never wanted to stick out or cause any trouble, I get it – being a part of an organization that is disruptive or confrontational may be outside of your comfort zone. It may feel risky. What are other people going to think about you if you join or take direct action? How will that affect your current relationships? What about your job? Also, this collective activism is time out of your day. And for what? Does it actually make a difference?

These concerns are real. But what's also real is that we are running out of time. And the tool that has proven, time and again, to be extremely effective at changing big systems relatively quickly (even when everyone thinks it's impossible to do so) is nonviolent civil resistance.

No matter who you are, there is almost certainly *something* you can do to support civil resistance campaigns. There are ways you can meaningfully contribute that make sense for you and your risk tolerance. People have found ways to engage in civil resistance for thousands of years (often people who are the most marginalized and under-resourced). So, if you haven't tried this kind of collective activism before, consider this an invitation to join our long line of courageous ancestors who struggled for a better future.

What Civil Resistance is and Why it Works

Civil resistance is when everyday people coordinate strikes, protests, sit-ins, boycotts, and other peaceful tactics to force change. It's what people turn to when the status quo is deadly and nothing else is working. It's a way for people to stop *asking* for change and start *demanding* it.

And it works remarkably well. When Harvard professor Erica Chenoweth and political scientist Maria Stephan studied 300+ resistance campaigns since 1900, they discovered that nonviolent campaigns are twice as effective as violent ones. And that when campaigns achieved the active participation of just 3.5% of the population, they succeeded 99% of the time.

But how and why does this nonviolent strategy work exactly? The answer lies in understanding what keeps any unjust system in power. So let's start with a visual. Picture the status quo as a roof held up by pillars:

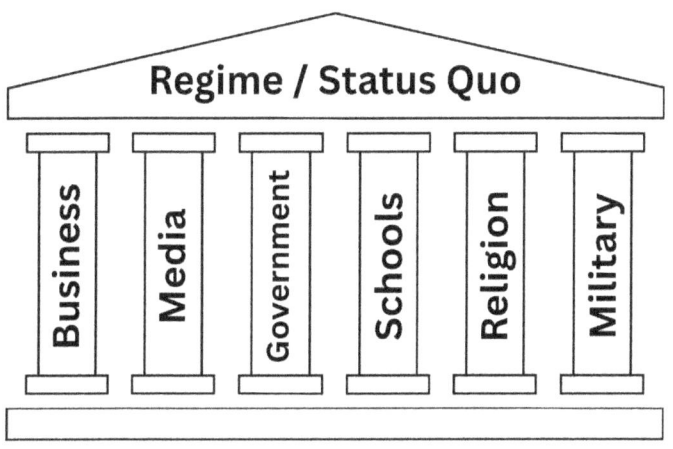

Pillars of Support. Credit: The Common's Library (modified)

As you can see, the status quo is held up by several institutions that give it legitimacy and serve as its "pillars of support" (e.g., business, media, schools). Without the cooperation and support of these pillars, the status quo would fall, providing an opportunity for something new to take its place. As Chenoweth says in their book *Civil Resistance*, "Masses of people change systems when, through popular collective action, they pull those pillars of support away from the power holder – the government, the university administration, the church – so as to disrupt or collapse an oppressive system."

Civil resistance campaigns are able to weaken or remove specific pillars because each pillar is made up of *people*. As social change campaigner Juman Abujbara writes in *Beautiful Rising*, "Power ultimately rests not in the grip of presidents, generals, and billionaires, but in the hands of millions of ordinary people who keep society running smoothly on a day-to-day basis, and who can shut it down should they so choose. … One of the main reasons that so many injustices persist is not that the powerful can simply do whatever they want with impunity, but that most people are ignorant of the power they can wield by withdrawing their consent."

When civil resistance campaigns gain traction, and people who are part of these pillars decide to side with the nonviolent civil resisters out of self-interest, the pillars begin to crumble. An example of this is when Dr. Martin Luther King Jr. co-organized the Birmingham campaign using boycotts, sit-ins, and marches to disrupt the status quo and weaken several pillars at once. Local businesses were hit hard by the boycotts, local jails were overwhelmed with student protesters, and pictures of the cruel response from law enforcement went viral in media worldwide. Seeing this, people across the country rose up and replicated the tactics in their respective cities, further weakening the pillars that upheld Jim Crow laws. This ultimately led to new local and national laws like the Voting Rights Act and the Civil Rights Act to end segregation and discriminatory hiring practices. And it all happened because the campaign had strategically built and exercised their people power, to the point where the people *in* power were forced to meet their demands.

In her book *Challenging Authority*, Professor Frances Fox Piven says that these are "extraordinary moments when [ordinary people] rise up in anger and hope, defy the rules that ordinarily govern their lives, and, by doing so, disrupt the workings of the institutions in which they are enmeshed. The drama of such events, combined with the disorder that results, propels new issues to the center of the political debate" and leads to reforms as "panicked political leaders try to restore order."

From Gandhi to Greta

Civil resistance has been used as a tactic to stand up to unjust power for about as far back as the historical record goes. From ancient Egypt to Haudenosaunee Clan Mothers to today, people have used it to stand up and leverage their collective power to change the way things are.

In 1930, Gandhi started a march with 78 people to peacefully protest an unjust British law forbidding Indians from making their own salt. By the time the Salt March reached the sea 24 days later, tens of thousands had joined to protest by making their own salt. This event was a turning point, helping to spark a movement that eventually led to Indian independence.

In 1955, Rosa Parks refused to give up her seat, which ignited the 13-month Montgomery bus boycott. This strategic campaign put immense economic pressure on local businesses and ultimately led to a Supreme Court case that declared segregation on buses unconstitutional – a key victory in the Civil Rights Movement.

In the 1950s, the Anti-Apartheid Movement was picking up steam in South Africa. Over decades, local boycotts on white businesses, international divestment and sanctions, and many more campaigns put immense pressure on the apartheid system. This pressure forced a change in leadership, reforms such as the right to vote for all citizens regardless of their race, and the release of Nelson Mandela from jail. He became President in the next election.

This. Stuff. Works.

As Chenoweth says, "Civil resistance is an increasingly common political approach, succeeding far more often than its detractors would have you believe. In fact, it's hard to find an example of progressive political change that occurred without it."

Today, the climate movement is utilizing the same playbook.

In 2018, the Sunrise Movement's civil resistance tactics helped popularize the Green New Deal and pressure politicians into supporting it. This ultimately helped lead to the largest climate bill ever being passed in the US, while also planting seeds for the European Green Deal and influencing policy in dozens of other cities, states, and countries.

In 2018, 15-year-old Greta Thunberg began a weekly school strike, protesting outside of Swedish Parliament to demand urgent action on climate change. Others soon joined her, creating a global movement called Fridays for Future. In September 2019, more than 7.5 million people took to the streets in 185 countries to demand climate action. Within three months, Scotland passed legislation to be net-zero by 2045, New Zealand passed a net-zero by 2050 target into law (3.5% of NZ's population participated in the strikes), and the European Commission passed the European Green Deal.

In 2021, the Great Sioux Nation, a coalition of Indigenous tribes, and environmental allies like 350, NRDC, and the Sierra Club defeated the Keystone XL pipeline after 13 years of organizing and resisting. Rights were upheld, land was protected, and 800,000 barrels of oil per day were prevented from flowing through the pipeline.

These are just a few of the campaigns weakening the pillars that support the status quo. And they show us what's possible when people take these courageous, collective actions.

To be honest, Covid disrupted the climate movement's momentum. But the climate crisis didn't pause – and neither can we. The organizations leading these campaigns need more support – more people power. And that's something we can all help with!

Keys to a Successful Civil Resistance Campaign

According to Chenoweth and Stephan's research, nonviolent civil resistance campaigns succeed when they:

1. Are big, diverse, and have sustained participation.
2. Get people in important positions (business, media, security forces) and other elites to shift to their side, or at least away from the status quo.
3. Use a variety of tactics beyond just protests like strikes, boycotts, and sit-ins (check out Gene Sharp's 198 Methods of Nonviolent Action for ideas).
4. Are disciplined and resilient, keeping their cool if the campaign is attacked rather than descending into chaos or responding with violence.

Additional research points to the importance of building momentum, creating alternative institutions, having clear and achievable demands, the ability to mobilize and scale in response to events, and the organizational capacity to engineer constructive disruption of their own.

When campaigns do these things, they pose a serious challenge to the status quo and are increasingly likely to win the changes they seek.

What You Can Do

As with so many actions, the main thing to do is to find your people! Most people and organizations in the climate movement aren't engaged in civil resistance yet, but a growing number are.

So ask around and search online to see if there are any climate organizations engaging in civil resistance in your area. Some organizations that might be active include 350.org, the Sunrise Movement, Extinction Rebellion, Fridays for Future, Third Act, and Greenpeace. If there's not a local chapter near you and you want to start one, reach out to one of these organizations – they will be happy to help you! Also keep your eyes open for local Indigenous communities that are defending their homes and ecosystems from fossil fuel pipelines, deforestation, and mining – these are always worthy efforts to support.

Once you find a group, go to the next meeting and start learning! What are they working on? Why? What are the specific goals and demands? Do they have a training you can go to?

Once you've wrapped your head around the basics, figure out how to support the campaign in a way that works for you. You don't have to put your body on the line or risk arrest if you don't want to. You can support them in almost any way you can think of.

As someone who was involved with the Sunrise Movement's influential DC protest for a Green New Deal in December 2018, I can tell you that *it took a village* to pull it off. My two main contributions were being willing to risk arrest and, get this, driving a van full of protestors from Boston to DC (because I was one of the only people old enough to drive the rented van). There were people who organized the event and all its logistics. There were people who filmed and amplified the protest on socials. There were people who trained those of us risking arrest. There were people who made art, taught us songs, and made things *fun*. There were friends and churches who gave us a place to sleep. There were people who made us food or bought us much appreciated pizza. There were media and police liaisons who were ready to talk to the press and police. There were those of us willing to peacefully risk arrest. And there were still more people waiting for us with snacks and rides when we got released.

What I'm trying to say is that there are *many* important roles. So if you want to help, there's always a way to lend a hand!

I also want to let you know that being involved in this kind of campaign can be a truly special experience (especially while singing, locking arms, and getting peacefully arrested). The mixture and depth of emotions – from belonging and determination to solidarity, pride, and hope – was something I'd never felt before. Being in these organizations is not always like that by any means. But when you're with people who know what's at stake and you're doing all that you can to move the world in the right direction together, there are some magical moments.

As you join these organizations or create these campaigns, don't be afraid to share your two cents on strategy – especially now that you know the keys to successful campaigns! Large protests are important, but to truly succeed, we need campaigns to deploy a variety of nonviolent, disruptive tactics. We need people to show up consistently. We need to grow the movement to be so large and diverse that it includes people in the pillars of support. We need to be disciplined and resilient when times get hard. And we need to stick together.

Finally, we need to come from a place of love – and create joy wherever we can along the way. Because that's what will keep us going – that's how we win.

"*Do not get lost in a sea of despair. Be hopeful, be optimistic. Our struggle is not the struggle of a day, a week, a month, or a year, it is the struggle of a lifetime. Never, ever be afraid to make some noise and get in good trouble, necessary trouble.*"

JOHN LEWIS, civil rights activist, politician

PART 4:
On Moving Forward Wisely

Here's the hard truth: even if we do everything right, the climate crisis is going to get worse before it gets better.

I don't say this to discourage you. I say it so we can be clear-eyed about the road ahead.

Because, despite positive momentum building, our broken systems are still actively making the planetary emergency worse. Until we stop polluting the climate, the world will keep getting hotter – the weather more extreme. And until we switch from harming ecosystems to healing them, ecological breakdown will continue. This means the world will become less habitable – harder to live in. It means all the important issues we care about – food security, housing, affordability, public health, racial equity, and so many others – will be made worse. And it means more people will suffer. More people will be displaced. And more people will die.

On the flip side, every action we take to burn less fossil fuels and restore ecosystems will make our air, food, and water cleaner – and the number of people dying every year from pollution that enters our hearts, brains, and lungs will start to decline.

Every bit we can do helps people in the present *and* lays the foundation for a better future that works for everyone. There's a lot of good work that needs to be done. By a lot of good people. Working together. Over a long period of time.

Which is why I want to end this book by getting back to basics and focusing on the intangibles we'll need to make it through the challenging decades ahead: taking care of ourselves and each other, changing our story, and remembering what matters most to us.

19. Taking Care of Ourselves & Each Other

No matter who you are or what you're doing, *you deserve care.*

But people working on climate, in particular, need to prioritize self-care because, as meaningful as this work is, it is also challenging and can be painful.

I know from experience how easy it can be to neglect your self-care and burn out (bad idea!). If you ever find yourself consistently prioritizing your impact over your well-being, just remember that you can't make the impact you want to if you're not healthy. You can't pour from an empty cup.

What taking care of yourself looks like will be a bit different for everyone. I'm by no means an expert, but some things that help me personally are making time for meditation, being with family and friends, practicing gratitude, playing soccer (any sport or game really), getting enough sleep, watching sunsets, long walks, delicious food, or being in nature. I think it's about a good mix of investing in your mental and physical health, relationships, fun, awe, spirituality if that's your thing, and ice cream (obviously).

Easier said than done, of course. And I am, and always will be, a work in progress. Though, for what it's worth, I've noticed that it's easier to spend more time on what fills you up if you first focus on subtracting what weighs you down (e.g., too much screen time).

Finally, a key piece of self-care is navigating your eco-emotions. As we talked about in Chapter 2, your challenging eco-emotions are *totally normal*. They're there for a reason and it's healthy to let yourself feel them.

When we acknowledge our feelings, connect with others who feel them, and start taking action together, not only do we begin to solve the root causes of the planetary emergency, but we also start living in a way that's more aligned with our values and start building something that is more important than ever: community.

Community

As important as self-care is, it's not enough on its own. We also need to take care of *each other*. We need community. Community is always important for living a full life (e.g., less loneliness, more connection, being a part of something bigger than ourselves). But it will be more important than ever in the turbulent decades ahead.

Why? Because climate and ecological breakdown will increasingly disrupt access to our basic necessities (e.g., food, water, healthcare, energy, shelter, jobs). These disruptions will make it harder for more and more of us to get by. For example, extreme weather and the declining health of soil and pollinators will lead to food shortages, struggling farmers, and higher prices. Coastal communities will face rising sea levels, along with more severe flooding and storms. Drier places will get drier and wetter places will get wetter, with more extreme droughts and floods. Insurance prices will go up everywhere. Heat waves will get worse. Healthcare services will be stretched thin. The power will go out more often and for longer. Supply chain disruptions will cause more shortages and higher prices on things we take for granted. I could go on and on with the impacts we know of, never mind the ones that we haven't thought of or seen yet.

When these events happen – when people are struggling and need support – we will have a choice to make: fear or love. We can turn *away* from each other or *toward* each other. We can respond to these mounting crises by doubling down on hyperindividualism (e.g., building walls, every person for themselves, etc.), or we can widen our circle of empathy, help each other get by, and work to solve our problems together. Hyperindividualism, supremacy, and domination got us into this mess. To get out of it, we need to do something different. We need to come together, treat each other with respect, and pool our resources to make our communities better and safer for everyone. Because there is no us and them – it's just us, sacred and interconnected beings.

The only way we will have the capacity to simultaneously weather the storms *and* build more regenerative, just, and resilient systems fast enough is if our communities come together and take care of each other. As author and activist Naomi Klein puts it, "The task is clear: to create a culture of caretaking in which no one and nowhere is thrown away – in which the inherent value of people and all life is foundational."

In practice, this could look like mutual aid networks, skill-sharing, tool libraries, repair cafes, communal fridges with free food – anything that supports people and prioritizes well-being.

Communities that embody this culture of care are built on strong relationships, trust, and shared values. Building a community like this means bringing people together and investing in relationships. It means having each other's backs and solving problems as a team. It means showing up, again and again, so our community networks grow stronger and become more tight-knit. With shared values, trust, and strong relationships, your community will be ready to quickly rise to the occasion and support people when they're in need – whether it's climate-related or not.

Investing in communities and networks like this is one of the most important actions we can take. Building relationships on trust, shared values, and shared experiences increases your community's power. This power not only helps you adapt to disruptions that come your way, but also build a better future together. Because when opportunities to shape policy and investment decisions arise, your community can more easily organize to influence them (e.g., by getting out the vote for an election, advocating at town hall meetings, or peacefully protesting).

Crucially – and this isn't talked about nearly enough – having more organized power to shape our communities also means the power to build more homes. Tens of millions of people are already being forced to leave their homes due to climate chaos today through no fault of their own. And that will go up to hundreds of millions of people (at least) in the decades to come. This is one of the things that breaks my heart the most. Everyone needs a good place to live. So, communities that are relatively safer climate-wise need to do what they can to build more sustainable housing and their overall capacity to welcome more people. And the countries and economic classes that are most responsible for causing these problems should do the most to help them.

Between making our communities pollution-free, resilient to extreme weather, and able to welcome more people, there is *a lot* that needs to be done. And accomplishing any or all of this life-saving and life-improving work starts with relationships and community. But we can do this. As Margaret Mead said, "Never doubt that a small group of thoughtful, committed citizens can change the world. Indeed, it's the only thing that ever has."

At the end of the day, community makes us more connected, more resilient, healthier, safer, and more fulfilled. Initiating and nurturing the intentional relationships that tight-knit communities require takes time and energy. But it's worth it. And absolutely necessary for this moment in time – because the reality is that climate chaos is here and getting worse. So we need to make our communities more resilient. And solve the problem at its roots.

The only question is: Will we face these big challenges alone? Or together?

20. Shifting the Paradigm

Collective change in our way of thinking and seeing things is crucial. Without it, we cannot expect the world to change.
THÍCH NHẤT HẠNH, Zen Master and peace activist

As we move forward, it's important to reflect on how we got here.

The most direct causes of the planetary emergency are clear, but what are the roots of the problem? How do we address them? And how do we learn from them so we don't repeat the same mistakes that got us into this mess?

This is where paradigms come in. Donella Meadows, a world-renowned systems educator and researcher, wrote that one of the most impactful ways to change a system is by shifting "the mindset or paradigm out of which the system – its goals, power structure, rules, its culture – arises." (You can also think of this as the *worldview* out of which the system arises.)

Shifting the paradigm means changing society's underlying assumptions of what is, what matters, and how things work. It's extremely powerful because changing these foundational assumptions affects every decision we make – ultimately reshaping our social and economic systems.

So the question is: how do we shift the paradigm?

It may seem an impossible task to change something so large and vague, but it all comes down to the stories we tell ourselves and each other every day. To understand this, we need to take a quick step back and look at humanity's underappreciated superpower.

For most of our existence, we Homo sapiens were somewhere in the middle of the food chain. Contrary to popular belief, it was not our big brains, tools, or mastery of fire that brought us to the top – no, our fellow human species (and yes, there were several) had those things too. What it was – what makes us special – is our ability to imagine, create, and believe in ideas that have no basis in reality. Think: nations, corporations, money.

As historian Yuval Noah Harari says, "We can create and believe fictional stories. And as long as everybody believes in the same fiction, everybody obeys and follows the same rules, the same norms, and the same values."

This ability to *collectively believe in ideas* – to create stories and fictitious entities that we've never seen, touched, or smelled – enabled us to cooperate flexibly with countless numbers of strangers and work together toward common goals.

This is our superpower.

But not all of the stories and beliefs from the past are accurate (shocking, I know). In fact, some of the most pervasive worldviews that shape our world today are so wildly *in*accurate – so out of touch with how the world actually works – that our social and economic systems are now at risk of collapsing if we don't change course.

As Dr. Elizabeth Sawin writes, "The dominant institutions of our world and the dominant cultures…are operating out of worldviews that don't actually match how the world works. And that's never going to lead to good results."

We know these worldviews don't work in the long run because the laws of nature are telling us that it's impossible to continue living on Earth as we do today. We didn't make up the laws of nature. And we can't change them. But we *did* make up these inaccurate stories that are destroying the foundations of civilization. And we *can* change them.

To get on the right track, we must identify the stories that led us astray and replace them with ones that more accurately reflect our values and how things work. Because when enough people stop believing the old story and start living a new one, entire systems transform.

To be clear, when I say 'stories,' I don't mean fiction or fairy tales. I mean the core beliefs that shape laws, direct investments, and justify actions. The story of white supremacy led to centuries of slavery and oppression. The story of manifest destiny justified genocide. Today, remnants of these inaccurate stories of supremacy are driving us toward collapse.

So what are they? And what new stories do we need?

Better Story #1: When We Harm Nature, We Harm Ourselves

This is true in the sense that poisoning the air we breathe, the water we drink, and the food we eat is bad for us. And it's true in the sense that harming nature destroys the very foundations we rely on – having enough food to eat, water to drink, and safe places to live. But it's also true on a deeper level. We, physically, atom for atom, came from and are made of the natural world we are harming. The oxygen in our lungs, the carbon in our DNA, the water in our blood – it all came from Mother Earth. Not too long ago, the atoms that make up our bodies were a part of rivers, clouds, forests, soil, mountains, the air, plants, animals…and one day they'll go back to them. These atoms are never created or destroyed, they just transform.

So, when we harm nature, we harm the mother that gave birth to all of us – Mother Earth. We harm everyone who's alive today. And we harm everyone who will be born in the future, for we are poisoning the air, water, and soil they will be made from and rely on.

But the dominant worldview doesn't recognize these truths yet. It views Earth and all our fellow beings as *less than* – as things that are there to be used and exploited. There is no respect, or gratitude, or awe.

But the reality is that this world is not ours *for the taking* – it's ours *to take care of*.

It's our home – the home of everyone and everything we love. So it's time to become more conscious of this interdependent reality and redesign our systems around it.

Better Story #2: People and Planet Matter More Than Profits

In today's world, society values GDP and quarterly earnings over people, health, education, justice, and the planet. We're told the economy matters more than the people's well-being it's *supposedly* an indicator of.

"Yes, the planet got destroyed. But for a beautiful moment in time we created a lot of value for shareholders."

Credit: Tom Toro. Reprinted with permission, CartoonStock.com

But we created money, government, and corporations so that *they* could serve *us* – not the other way around. And it's long past time for the masses to reassert our power over them – to use them as tools that reflect our shared values and help us achieve our shared goals.

> "When the last tree is cut, the last fish is caught, and the last river is polluted; when to breathe the air is sickening, you will realize, too late, that wealth is not in bank accounts and that you can't eat money."
> **ALANIS OBOMSAWIN**, Abenaki filmmaker and activist

Embodying The Shift

Climate and ecological breakdown are symptoms of a deeper problem. They're symptoms of inaccurate stories about how the world works, our place in it, and what matters most to us.

But stories can change. And when they do, entire worldviews shift with them.

If you feel like it's impossible for people to tell and live by more life-centered stories, just remember: people already have, and do. None of this is new – it's quite old actually. Many Indigenous peoples have lived by worldviews that center life and interconnectedness for thousands of years. An eye-opening example of this we can all take to heart immediately is the contrast in what it means to be a "warrior." In her book *Sacred Instructions*, Sherri Mitchell shares what it meant to be a warrior:

> "In most ancient warrior traditions, being a warrior related to a very specific code of conduct that involved respect, honor, protection, and service. In the Wabanaki tradition, being a warrior meant that you were both a helper and a shield to the community. … [Warriors] do not hesitate to speak the truth about issues that pose a threat to the well-being of the people and the continuity of life. Yet they do so in ways that demonstrate respect for those they are addressing. … A warrior must be respectful and disciplined in their interactions with all living beings and committed to protecting the sacredness of every life."

As caretakers committed to protecting the land, people, and future generations, these warriors are role models for all of us. And we need peaceful armies of them everywhere.

The good news is that we are ready for this change. Everyone knows the status quo is broken. Our hearts are calling for systems that actually align with our values. Because deep down we all know that *life* is sacred, not money or power. That we are *interdependent*, not independent. That we are a part *of* nature, not apart *from* nature. And that *everyone* should get a fair shot and be treated with dignity.

This is the paradigm shift we need: from warriors of domination to warriors of protection. From stories of separation to stories of connection. From systems that take life to systems that *give* life.

So how do we shift the paradigm? By embodying the principles of these peace-oriented warriors and taking the actions in Part 3. Every time you speak the truth about threats to life, every time you stand up for what's right, every time you take action to protect all beings – you embody, and spread, the new story.

And that's how the paradigm shifts. One story, one person, one action at a time.

> *"The time has come for us to re-imagine everything...to become the new kind of people that are needed at such a huge period of transition."*
>
> GRACE LEE BOGGS, social activist, visionary

21. What Matters Most?

I think, especially if you've made it this far in the book, you have an intuition – a gut feeling. You know that this is something you *want* to be doing more of.

And I'm here to tell you to *just f****** go for it*.

Just take that next step – whatever that means for you. Maybe that means committing to leveling up your action and taking the time to find your place in the movement. Maybe it means shifting gears from reducing your footprint to improving a larger system like your company or town with the people around you. Maybe it means doing that big, bold, courageous thing you've been wanting to do for a long time but have held back on for one reason or another.

Whatever it is – whatever that next step is for you – now is the time to take it. Now is the time for us to get out of our comfort zones and do more. Now is the time to be brave – even if it feels scary. Courage isn't about being fearless – it's about taking action despite your fear because you know something matters more.

So just start. Talk to people. Connect. Work together. Try new things. Fail. Learn. Laugh. Figure it out. Celebrate your wins. Take care of yourself. And keep going.

Take the first step. Then the next one. And the next. Your only regret will be that you didn't start sooner.

You might be thinking, "But won't this make my life harder?" In some ways, yes – you'll stretch your comfort zone. But this isn't as hard a decision as we sometimes make it out to be, because what's killing the planet is also killing our quality of life.

And when we improve the planet, we improve our quality of life.

Climate Action Makes Your Life Better

Some people turn away from climate action because they think ignoring the problem makes their life better. They're wrong. I think part of living a good, full life means you turn *toward* climate action. What is good about being a part of a status quo that actively harms yourself and others? What is good about lying to yourself that you don't care or that there's nothing you can do? What is good about living out of alignment with your values?

Gandhi famously taught that happiness is when what you think, what you say, and what you do are in harmony.

Billions of people are worried about climate and ecological breakdown. Billions of us say more needs to be done to address it. And billions of us want to personally do more to help. In other words, what billions of us are *thinking* and *saying* is not in harmony with what we're *doing*.

That means there is friction in our lives – misalignment – we're not being the people we want to be. And I think, deep down, this is because we see ourselves as good people (and we are). But given the situation we're in, being good requires more of us now than it used to. Because protecting the people and places we love means *taking action* to change the systems that are currently killing life on Earth.

Aligning our values, words, and actions is, of course, key to happiness. But taking action on climate also makes our lives better in so many other ways. It leads to less loneliness and more community. Less anxiety and more peace. Less emptiness and more meaning.

We can choose to be part of the problem or part of the solution. And the solution has so much more *life* and *love* and *meaning* and *connection*.

The bottom line is: we don't have to choose between helping ourselves and helping the world – we can do both. When we help save and improve lives, we help save and improve our own.

Our Moment In Time

> *"The climate emergency is not an issue, it's an era. It's **when** we live."*
> ALEX STEFFEN

We're at an inflection point. The climate and ecosystems that are foundational to our existence are collapsing. And more and more people now see that the worldviews and systems that got us into this mess are not working – that something better is needed. Taken together, systemic change isn't impossible – it's inevitable. And what it looks like is up to us.

To avoid crossing environmental tipping points and the worst impacts of the planetary emergency, we need to work to reach the positive, social tipping points for systemic change as quickly and equitably as possible. When enough people step up to activate the good tipping points in our social and economic systems, we'll start transforming much faster than we tend to think is possible.

But this change won't happen overnight – and it may not seem like it's coming at all. As disability rights activist Judy Heumann said, "Change never happens at the pace we think it should. It happens over years of people joining together, strategizing, sharing, and pulling all the levers they possibly can. Gradually, excruciatingly slowly, things start to happen, and then suddenly, seemingly out of the blue, something will tip."

All we need is persistence and people power. We need enough people like you and me to show up, again and again, to do what we can to build a world where all of life thrives. Because every school, town, and company needs to change. And as people who belong to and know people in these places, we are the only ones who can change them.

I know this isn't going to be easy. And how long it takes to change things can be discouraging. But as Dr. Elizabeth Sawin says, "Hang on to the possibility that we may be closer to transformation than we realize. Just keep going because you really don't know."

We likely *are* closer to transformation than we realize. But even if we weren't – even if it was really far off – even if we knew we'd never get to fully experience the better world we're building in our lifetime – I believe you and I will do our best to push for it anyway. Because this is not just about **when** we are in time. It's also about **who** we are as people. It's about what matters most to us.

I started this book by sharing my *Truths and Life Intentions*. I'm going to end it by sharing the questions that led to it: What would you do if you had just one minute left to live? One day? One year? One decade?

These questions get at something that's unbelievably important but can easily get lost in our busy lives: We only get one life. And we don't know when it's going to end.

How do you want to live yours? What matters most to you? What does a good life look like? And what can you do to spend the time you have left living closer to how you actually want to live?

This is what climate action is all about. It's about cherishing our relationships with each other and our time on this Earth. It's about being the people we want to be and making the world a better place. It's an expression of our love – an expression of *who we are*.

If you're honest with yourself about the situation and your values and choose not to act on climate, that's fine. But at least do the reflecting and be true to who you are and what you care about. Because that's what we'll all judge ourselves by on our deathbeds: Did I live true to myself, my values, and what mattered most to me?

Increasingly, these reflections will also happen before our deathbeds. They'll happen in a quiet moment with someone we love. A child – your child, your grandchild, your niece or nephew. A child who is growing up in a world of climate chaos. A child who will learn about these pivotal years in school. And they'll ask you: "Did you know? Did you know it was happening and how bad it was gonna be?"

And, after you answer, the second, more important question will follow: "What did you do?"

Whatever you do after closing this book, always remember that you matter. That you are not alone. That we have the solutions. That you are more powerful than you think. And that your actions will have more positive ripple effects than you'll ever know.

Thank you for being you and for all that you do.

Much love,

Ryan

Thank You & A Quick Climate Action

Thank you for reading! I really hope this book has helped you on your climate journey.

And I hope it helps a lot more people like you. I wrote it to accelerate climate action in towns, cities, schools, and organizations around the world. But the only way it can do that is if it gets into the hands of the people who are a part of these places.

So, if you found this book valuable and want to take a quick climate action now, I'd really appreciate it if you:

1. Write an honest review

It'd mean a lot to me if you wrote a review for this book while it's still fresh (even just a sentence or two is awesome!). This makes a big difference because it helps more people to find and get the book, building our people power.

To make it as easy as possible, consider answering one of these questions:

- Who would you recommend this book to?
- What was your biggest takeaway?
- How has (or will) this book help you on your journey?

And feel free to write it wherever you'd like – the most impactful place, however, is likely Amazon or Goodreads:

https://bit.ly/ClimateActionReviewAmazon
https://bit.ly/ClimateActionGoodreads

2. Share the book!

Give your copy to a friend, recommend it to your local library, or give it as a gift! Thank you again for helping to get this guide into more people's hands – I really appreciate your support and the positive ripple effects it will have!!

Acknowledgments

I want to start by thanking you. As you'll see, it took a village of amazing people giving their time, support, and feedback to make this book. But it only exists because there are good people like you who want to make our world a better place. So thank you for being you, for reading, for sharing what you've learned with others, and for all the great things you'll do going forward.

Family & Friends

To my family: Mom, Dad, Tyler, Nicki, Gran, Grammy, Grandpa, and everyone else – I love you. Your love means so much to me. And I wouldn't be who I am today without you and your unwavering support, encouragement, and belief in me, so thank you.

To my friends: whether you directly helped with this book or not, thank you. I literally started smiling as I wrote "to my friends" and memories started flashing through my head. So grateful for all of you, all your support, and all the good times we've shared together.

Where it Started

To everyone who was a part of and supported Crowdsourcing Sustainability, thank you. Whether you were a reader, donor, or gave us grants (thank you Woka Foundation and Forest Foundation!), you helped set the 5-year foundation of research, writing, and community-building that this book was built on.

To Chad Frischmann, Amanda Joy Ravenhill, Ryan Allard, and the whole Regenerative Intelligence team – thank you for helping me decide to write this book in the first place, for giving feedback on the earliest outlines, and for generously sharing your time and wisdom.

Editors & Early Readers

To my editor Larry Yu, thank you for your crucial feedback that helped make everything flow more naturally, for your patience with my unorthodox style, and for being a good thought partner. Thank you to Brendan Burke for your meticulous proofreading and being an insightful sounding board. And to my first editors: Mom and Dad.

To Nicki, Jack Hanson, Abby Shepard, Rachel Malena-Chan, Patrick Kelley, Emily Baksa, Rachel Wiley, Benoit Denizet-Lewis, Almy Landaeur, and Tom Garvey – thank you for reading the early (and rough) drafts of this book. Your valuable feedback and ideas helped get this thing into shape! And to Rachel Taylor, for editing the original newsletters that were the starting point for a couple chapters.

Cover, Design, Title, Images

To Elizabeth Edwards, thank you for making this such a beautiful book both inside and out. I love it and am so grateful to have gotten to work with you. Sabatina Leccia, thank you for sharing your gorgeous art for the cover – it really makes it! To Brad Gake and Kristin Hagen – thank you for drawing the people on their climate journey – they are all of us! And a big thank you to everyone who gave feedback on the cover and title!

Thank you to everyone who let me use their images (with a special shoutout to Kāya Pulz, Jane Morton, Ayana Elizabeth Johnson and Joel Pett!) – this book wouldn't be the same without them.

Expert Reviewers

To all the experts who generously gave their time to read specific chapters and give feedback: Andrew Dessler, Chad Frischmann, Britt Wray, Rachel Malena-Chan, Daniel Elledge, Assaad Razzouk, Ed Maibach, Roberta Bosu, Nathaniel Stinnett, Jack Hanson, Quinton Zondervan, Heidi Frail, Marc Anthonisen, Adrienne Greve, Bill Weihl, Holly Alpine, Aiyana Bodi, Kevin Houldsworth, Lucy Piper, Eddie Galvin, Daniel Hill, Shiva Rajbhandari, Ben Langton, Eliza Nemser, Jamie Henn, Breene Murphy, Jackie Francis – thank you!

Your feedback was extremely helpful and made this book so much more useful for everyone who reads it. And a big thanks to all the researchers and experts who answered specific questions about their studies, statistics, and quotes – I am so grateful for your help!

Kickstarter Supporters

And a special thank you to everyone who helped bring this book to life by supporting the Kickstarter:

Abby Shepard, Adam Dings, Alex Norman, Allison, Amber Baur, Amir Haghighat, Amy Gerber, Angela Parnay, Ann Schneider, Anna Chirico, Anna Maassel, Anthea Lawrence, Anthony Capraro, Arthur Gavrilles, Ben Bolton, Betsy Franco-Feeney, Bob Neer, Bou Piscaer, Brad Gake, Brendan Burke, Brian B., Brian Galvin, Brian Nadler, Brian O'Keefe, Brianna Kennedy, Camden Francis, Carol Kinlan, Caron Peacock, Chris Bell, Christine Dinneen, Chuck Tomaselli, Claire Schoen, Conor Galvin, Cory Humphreys Serrano, Craig Galvin, Daniel Alpert, Daniel Elledge, Daniela Arias, Danny Galvin, David Burr, Deborah Matherly, Deirdre Morris, Denise Baden, Diana Yu Rewinski, Dominique Lim, Doris Hagen, Doug Schneider, Eddie Galvin, Emily Baksa, Eric Lowenstein, Fran Ludwig, Gabby Krause, Geraldine Garrs, Gerry Galvin, Glenn Shapiro, Greg, Greg Kinlan, Gregg Servheen, Griffen Fargo, H W Hagen, Hannah Hausman, Hannah Muhlfelder, Hans Hagen, Hans van Wijngaarden, Hillary Adams, Jack Hanson, Jackie Giovanniello, Jake Graff, James C Mulloy, Jeff Szot, Jennifer L Ferriss, Jessica Groopman, Jessica Serrante, Jon Leland, Joachim Weber, Joao, John Messina, Jon Wellman, Joseph DeNatalie, Josh Nadler, Joshua Kibbey, JP Wade, Judy Campbell, Judy Holm, Kai Martin, Katharina Meyer, Kelly Portelli, Kerry Hecker, Kevin Thorley, Krista Kurth, Kristiina Almy, Kyle G. Crider, Larry Yu, Lindsay Guerriere, Patricia Bullis, Maia Sallouti, Máire Ní Ghealbháin, Marilyn and Bob Brooks, Marin Redfield, MaryBeth Mittaz, Maryann Ryan, Matt Alfano, Matt Bray, Matt Daly, Matt Halliday, Matt Neckes, Matt Seeger, Matthew Elman, Meghan Murphy, Meike, Melinda Kucsera, Michael Potts, Mike Galvin, Mike Moran, Mitche, Monivann Lor, Mordanti, Nancy Jane Sevitz-Poarch, Nancy Richter, Nate Rauh-Bieri, Netri Kalra, Nicki Hagen, Nikki T.,

Noreen Capraro, PaintBe inc., Patrice Hagen, Patrick Kelley, Paul Agranat, Paul Shorthose, Peg Galvin, Peter & Kerry Gould, Phil Francisco, Phill Tuxford, PJ Mensel, Rachel Wiley, Ralph Cassar, Reilley Keane, Rhiannon Drummond-Clark, Robert Capron, Robert Connors, Roberta Bosu, Roh James, Ryan McNamara, Ryan Woolley, Sam Dushay, Sam Levac-Levey, Sam Vincoli-Miyamoto, Samuel-Louis Gardiner, Sandy, Sarah Hanson, Sarah Tabor, Sean Koljonen, Shikha Bhurtel, Sigurdur Jonatansson, Stan Brinkerhoff, Steve Dickison, Steve Seremeth, Susan Hunt Stevens, Suzanne Hamner, Taylor, The High Frontier, Thomas Garvey, Tom Quinn, Tyler Hagen, Tyler Stacey, Willy Bliss, Zach Agranat, and Zack Arthus

You are all amazing. Thank you for helping to make this book what it is and for all that you do!

Many More!

There are many other people who I would like to give a big thank you to as well for how they have helped shape my thinking over the years: Alex Steffen, Amy Westervelt, Amanda Joy Ravenhill, Ayana Elizabeth Johnson, Bill McKibben, Carl Sagan, David Roberts, Elizabeth Sawin, Emily Atkin, Greta Thunberg, James Hansen, Jess Serrante, Jigar Shah, Joanna Macy, Katharine Wilkinson, Mary Annaïse Heglar, Mitzi Jonelle Tan, Renée Lertzman, Saul Griffith, Sherri Mitchell, Varshini Prakash. To all my teachers – especially sustainability professors: Paul Rosier, Francis Galgano, Michael Freeman, Ed Guinan, Bonnie Henderson, Liesel Schwarz. To every guest who shared their wisdom on the Crowdsourcing Sustainability podcast. And to many more lovely, smart people who I've connected with over the years – thank you :)

Resources & Citations

If you'd like a version of this with links, plus bonus lists of my favorite climate books, newsletters, podcasts, and documentaries, visit: https://bit.ly/ClimateActionResources

PREFACE
Sawin quote Sawin, Elizabeth. "Feedback Loops and Climate Catastrophe." *Crazy Town*, episode 45, Post Carbon Institute, June 9, 2021.

INTRODUCTION
Billions worried United Nations Development Programme. *The Peoples' Climate Vote 2024*. 2024. **Billions want to do more** American Psychological Association. "Majority of US Adults Believe Climate Change Is Most Important Issue Today." 2020.
Future pathways chart Urban, Tim. "How Covid Stole Our Time and How We Can Get It Back." *The New York Times*, February 25, 2022.
Insurance fueling climate crisis Bosshard, Peter. *Within Our Power: Cut Emissions Today to Insure Tomorrow*. Insure Our Future, 2023.

CHAPTER 1
This is water story Wallace, David Foster. *This Is Water*. Little, Brown and Company, 2009.
Climate changing faster NASA. "Evidence - NASA Science." Climate Change, June 15, 2022.
Ten times faster than deadliest mass extinction Wu, Yuyang, et al. "Volcanic CO_2 Degassing Postdates Thermogenic Carbon Emission during the End-Permian Mass Extinction." *Science Advances* 9, no. 7 (2023).
2.6 trillion tonnes Evans, Simon. "Analysis: Which Countries Are Historically Responsible for Climate Change?" Carbon Brief, October 5, 2021.
Nature absorbed 56% of CO_2 emissions + 50% increase in atmospheric CO_2 Friedlingstein, Pierre, et al. "Global Carbon Budget 2024." *Earth System Science Data* 17, no. 3 (2025).
Weight of all life and man-made stuff Elhacham, Emily, et al. "Global Human-Made Mass Exceeds All Living Biomass." *Nature* 588, no. 7838 (2020).
Populations…declined by 73% WWF. *Living Planet Report 2024*. 2024.
Earth has heated by 1.4°C World Meteorological Organization (WMO). *Global*

Annual to Decadal Climate Update (2025-2029). 2025.
2.7°C heating Climate Action Tracker. "2100 Warming Projections." November 2024.
President Johnson's advisors President's Science Advisory Council. "Restoring the Quality of Our Environment." November 1965. **Exxon's scientists**: Inside Climate News. "Exxon: The Road Not Taken." September 15, 2015. **Sagan's testimony**: *Carl Sagan Testifying before Congress in 1985 on Climate Change*. YouTube, 2021. **Hansen's testimony:** Shabecoff, Philip. "Global Warming Has Begun, Expert Tells Senate." *The New York Times*, June 24, 1988.
Shell report Shell Confidential Planning Group. *Scenarios 1989-2010, Challenge and Response*. Shell, 1989.
We Are Here chart Morton, Jane. *Don't Mention The Emergency?* 2020. (*Originally based on a chart by Jos Hagalaars with data from various scientific papers, updated by Morton's team for the book.*)
3 million years ago CO_2, temps, sea levels Intergovernmental Panel On Climate Change (IPCC). *Climate Change 2021: The Physical Science Basis*. Cambridge University Press, 2023.
Trillions $ at risk on coast Xu, Jiayi. *2025 Realtor.com Housing and Climate Risk Report*. Realtor.com, 2025.
Staple crops decline IPCC. *Climate Change 2022: Impacts, Adaptation and Vulnerability*. Cambridge University Press, 2023.
2.5 billion farm for livelihood Food and Agriculture Organization of the United Nations (FAO). *Increasing the Resilience of Agriculture Livelihoods to Threats and Crises*. 2016.
3 billion people rely on seafood World Wildlife Fund. "Sustainable Seafood." Accessed August 25, 2025.
Wildfires burn 2x acres Congressional Research Service. "Wildfire Statistics." September 7, 2023.
⅓ in US live with high fire risk Canon, Gabrielle, and Andrew Witherspoon. "Millions of Americans Believe They're Safe from Wildfires in Their Cities. New Research Shows They're Not." *The Guardian*, April 5, 2025.
Heat makes ground ozone worse Shen, L., L. J. Mickley, and E. Gilleland. "Impact of Increasing Heat Waves on U.S. Ozone Episodes in the 2050s." *Geophysical Research Letters* 43, no. 8 (2016).
Phytoplankton struggling Zhang, Yukun, John Beardall, and Kunshan Gao. "Combined Effects of Ocean Acidification and Warming on Phytoplankton Productivity." *Marine Environmental Research* 210 (2025).
CO river flows declining Udall, Bradley, and Jonathan Overpeck. "The Twenty-first Century Colorado River Hot Drought and Implications for the Future." *Water Resources Research* 53, no. 3 (2017).
60% of freshwater, glaciers United Nations. *The United Nations World Water*

Development Report 2025: Mountains and Glaciers*. 2025.
Saltwater contaminating fresh water supplies Adams, Kyra H., et al. "Climate-Induced Saltwater Intrusion in 2100." *Geophysical Research Letters* 51, no. 22 (2024).
2.4 billion outdoor workers International Labor Organization. *Ensuring Safety and Health at Work in a Changing Climate*. 2024.
Ticks, mosquitoes, pandemics Wu, Xiaoxu, et al. "Impact of Climate Change on Human Infectious Diseases." *Environment International* 86 (2016).
Exceeded 7/9 planetary boundaries Stockholm Resilience Centre, et al. Planetary Health Check 2025. 2025.
45 million forced to leave home Internal Displacement Monitoring Centre. *2025 Global Report on Internal Displacement*. 2025.
Possibly 1.2 billion displaced by 2050 Institute for Economics & Peace. *Ecological Threat Register 2020*. September 2020.
Pakhi's story Simonsson, Otto. "'I Did It Only for the Money': Climate Displacement Pushes Girls into Prostitution." Reuters, October 17, 2018.
1/500 year Syrian drought Ash, Konstantin, and Nick Obradovich. "Climatic Stress, Internal Migration, and Syrian Civil War Onset." *Journal of Conflict Resolution* 64, no. 1 (2020).
600,000 & 13 million Syrian Observatory for Human Rights. "Syrian Revolution 13 Years on | Nearly 618,000 Persons Killed." March 15, 2024.
Tipping points chart Data: Armstrong McKay, David I., et al. "Exceeding 1.5°C Global Warming Could Trigger Multiple Climate Tipping Points." *Science* 377, no. 6611 (2022). (Image by PIK/GLOBAÏA, slightly modified).
Lenton quote Lenton, Tim. *La Figure Scientifique de Gaïa*. YouTube, 2020. (Quote at 44:25).
Steinberger quote Steinberger, Julia. In "*MONBIOSIS with George Monbiot: Ep5 - Scientists Speaking Out*." YouTube, 2022. (Quote at 4:08).
Baldwin quote Baldwin, James. "AS MUCH TRUTH AS ONE CAN BEAR." *The New York Times*, January 14, 1962.

CHAPTER 2

Wray quote Wray, Britt. *Generation Dread: Finding Purpose in an Age of Climate Anxiety*. The Experiment, 2023.
Fossil fuel industry spent billions Brulle, Robert J. "The Climate Lobby: A Sectoral Analysis of Lobbying Spending on Climate Change in the USA, 2000 to 2016." *Climatic Change* 149, (2018): 289-303.
Klein quote Klein, Naomi. *This Changes Everything: Capitalism vs. the Climate*. Simon & Schuster, 2014.
Wray quote Wray, Britt. "What It Feels like to Rouse Painfully Awkward Emotions with Fossil Fuel Executives." *Unthinkable*, October 2, 2020.

Macy quote Macy, Joanna. *World As Lover, World As Self*. Parallax Press, 2021.
Sawin quote Crowdsourcing Sustainability. "Systems Change, Multisolving, and the Power to Change Direction with Dr. Elizabeth Sawin." YouTube, September 9, 2021. (Quote at 01:03:20).
Name it to tame it Siegel, Daniel J., and Tina Payne Bryson. *The Whole-Brain Child: 12 Revolutionary Strategies to Nurture Your Child's Developing Mind*. Random House, 2011.
Wray "sweet spot" quote Wray, Britt. "Why Emotionally Intelligent Climate Work Matters." *Unthinkable*, January 6, 2021.
True antidote to despair Wray, Britt. *Generation Dread*. The Experiment, 2023.
The Work That Reconnects workthatreconnects.org
We Are the Great Turning podcast resources.soundstrue.com/we-are-the-great-turning-podcast
The All We Can Save Project's Circles allwecansave.earth/circles
The Good Grief Network goodgriefnetwork.org
The Unthinkable Newsletter gendread.substack.com/about
Eco-Anxious Stories ecoanxious.ca/resources
Project Inside Out projectinsideout.net
Hundreds of millions may take more action Leiserowitz, Anthony, et al. "Climate Change in the American Mind: Beliefs & Attitudes, Fall 2023." Yale Program on Climate Change Communication, 2023.
Macy quote Amity Foundation. "Awakening the Dreamer: Changing the Dream." YouTube, 2020. (Quote at 59:42).

CHAPTER 3

McKibben quote McKibben, Bill. "In a World on Fire, Stop Burning Things." *The New Yorker*, March 18, 2022.
1.5 to stay alive Alliance of Small Island States. "Small Islands Propose 'below 1.5°C' Global Goal for Paris Agreement."
Limiting heating to 1.5°C IPCC. *Global Warming of 1.5°C*. Cambridge University Press, 2022.
1.4°C World Meteorological Organization (WMO). *Global Annual to Decadal Climate Update (2025-2029)*. 2025.
2.7°C Climate Action Tracker. "2100 Warming Projections." November 2024.
Frischmann quote Frischmann, Chad. "100 Solutions to Reverse Global Warming." TED Talk, September 2018.
57.4 billion tonnes United Nations Environment Programme. *Emissions Gap Report 2024*. 2024.
75% emissions from fossil fuels United Nations. "Causes and Effects of Climate Change." Accessed August 26, 2025.
Other 25% from food, ag, deforestation, industry IPCC. "Emissions Trends

and Drivers." In *Climate Change 2022: Mitigation of Climate Change*. Cambridge University Press, 2023.
GHG sources chart Project Drawdown. "Drawdown® Roadmap."
Nature sequestering 41% of emissions Project Drawdown. *The Drawdown Review: Climate Solutions for a New Decade*. 2020.
Nature's capacity to sequester carbon declining IPCC. *Climate Change 2022: Impacts, Adaptation and Vulnerability*. Cambridge University Press, 2023.
Need to sequester 100s of billions IPCC. "Mitigation Pathways Compatible with Long-Term Goals." In *Climate Change 2022: Mitigation of Climate Change*. Cambridge University Press, 2023.
Solutions chart Project Drawdown. "Drawdown® Roadmap."
Trillions cost and savings for 1.5, 2°C Project Drawdown. *The Drawdown Review: Climate Solutions for a New Decade*. 2020.
$2 trillion invested in climate solutions annually, $6 trillion needed Climate Policy Initiative. *Global Landscape of Climate Finance 2025*. 2025.
Citizens' Climate Lobby's carbon fee & dividend https://citizensclimatelobby.org/basics-carbon-fee-dividend/
Time value of carbon chart Project Drawdown. "Drawdown® Roadmap."
Burning all fossil fuels = 8-10°C heating Tokarska, Katarzyna B., et al. "The Climate Response to Five Trillion Tonnes of Carbon." *Nature Climate Change* 6, no. 9 (2016).
Carney quote Shankleman, Jessica. "Mark Carney: Most Fossil Fuel Reserves Can't Be Burned." *The Guardian*, October 13, 2014.
No new fossil fuel development International Energy Agency. *Net Zero by 2050*. 2021.
Hundreds of billions invested in fossil fuels Rainforest Action Network, BankTrack, Indigenous Environmental Network, Oil Change International, Reclaim Finance, Sierra Club, Urgewald, and CEED. *Banking on Climate Chaos 2025*. 2025.
Production Gap Report Stockholm Environment Institute, et al. *The Production Gap 2023*. 2023.
Fossil Fuel Non-Proliferation Treaty fossilfueltreaty.org
Trillions of dollars of FF in ground Lewis, Mark C. *Stranded Assets, Fossilised Revenues*. Kepler Cheuvreux, 2014.
Cartoon Pett, Joel. "What if it's a big hoax…" Cartoon. *USA Today*, December 7, 2009.
Sawin quote Crowdsourcing Sustainability. "Systems Change, Multisolving, and the Power to Change Direction with Dr. Elizabeth Sawin." YouTube, September 9, 2021.
Air pollution from FF kills 8.7 million/year Vohra, Karn, et al. "Global Mortality from Outdoor Fine Particle Pollution Generated by Fossil Fuel

Combustion." *Environmental Research* 195 (2021).
Heart disease, lung disease, stroke, lung cancer World Health Organization. "9 out of 10 People Worldwide Breathe Polluted Air, but More Countries Are Taking Action." May 2, 2018.
FF pollution takes 1 year off our lives Lelieveld, Jos, et al. "Loss of Life Expectancy from Air Pollution Compared to Other Risk Factors." *Cardiovascular Research* 116, no. 11 (2020).
Air pollution harms babies in womb Aguilera, Juan, et al. "Air Pollution and Pregnancy." *Seminars in Perinatology* 47, no. 8 (2023).
Impacts disproportionately affect people of color Tessum, Christopher W., et al. "PM2.5 Polluters Disproportionately and Systemically Affect People of Color in the United States." *Science Advances* 7, no. 18 (2021).
health savings from getting off of fossil fuels far outweigh transition cost World Health Organization. "Health Benefits Far Outweigh the Costs of Meeting Climate Change Goals." December 5, 2018.

CHAPTER 4

Russell quote Russell, Cormac. "Sustainable Community Development: From What's Wrong to What's Strong." TEDxExeter, May 16, 2016.
Climate movement arguably biggest in history Global Climate Strike. "7.6 Million People Demand Action after Week of Climate Strikes." September 28, 2019.
67% see climate as a major threat Poushter, Jacob, et al. "Global Climate Change as a Threat." Pew Research Center, August 19, 2025.
89% of people want more action UNDP Climate Promise. "The World's Largest Survey on Climate Change Is out - Here's What the Results Show." June 20, 2024.
"the cheapest source of electricity in history" International Energy Agency. *World Energy Outlook 2020.* 2020.
Solar and wind cheaper than FF over 90% of the time International Renewable Energy Agency. *Renewable Power Generation Costs in 2024.* 2025.
41% of world's electricity zero-carbon sources Graham, Euan, Nicolas Fulghum, and Katye Altiere. *Global Electricity Review 2025.* Ember, 2025.
Battery costs down 84% Graham, Euan, Nicolas Fulghum, and Katye Altiere. *Global Electricity Review 2025.* Ember, 2025.
Gas car sales peaked International Energy Agency. *World Energy Outlook 2023.* 2023.
$2.2 trillion clean energy investments International Energy Agency. *World Energy Investment 2025.* 2025.
Emissions peaked in ~50 countries Levin, K., and D. Rich. "Turning Points: Trends in Countries' Reaching Peak Greenhouse Gas Emissions over Time." World Resources Institute, 2017.

China may peak emissions in 2025 Myllyvirta, Lauri. "Analysis: Clean Energy Just Put China's CO_2 Emissions into Reverse for First Time." Carbon Brief, May 14, 2025.

Global emissions expected to peak in late 2020s International Energy Agency. *World Energy Outlook 2023.* 2023.

European green deal $1 trillion European Commission. "The European Green Deal Investment Plan and JTM Explained." Accessed August 28, 2025.

13,770 local governments "Global Covenant of Mayors." Accessed August 28, 2025.

2,350 jurisdictions have declared an emergency Aidt, Mik. "Climate Emergency Declarations in 2,366 Jurisdictions and Local Governments Cover 1 Billion Citizens." Climate Emergency Declaration, March 24, 2025.

Thousands of lawsuits "Climate Lawsuits Are On The Rise. This Is What They're Based On." State of the Planet, August 9, 2023.

11,000 corporations Science Based Targets Initiative. *SBTi Trend Tracker 2025.* 2025.

$40 trillion divesting from fossil fuels "Homepage - Global Fossil Fuel Commitments Database." Accessed August 28, 2025.

CHAPTER 5

Hubbard quote Widely attributed to Barbara Marx Hubbard (though I can't track down the original source).

Andretti quote Clear, James. "Haters and Critics: How to Deal with People Judging You and Your Work." JamesClear.com, September 16, 2013.

Doughnut economics image "The Doughnut of social and planetary boundaries". Credit: Kate Raworth and Christian Guthier. CC-BY-SA 4.0. Raworth, K. (2017), *Doughnut Economics: seven ways to think like a 21st century economist.* London: Penguin Random House.

Image: Spot the car, spot the horse "Picturing the Century | A New Century Gallery." National Archives, 1900; and Library of Congress. "5th Ave. - Easter, '13." Image.

CHAPTER 6

Mead quote Lutkehaus, Nancy C. *Margaret Mead: The Making of an American Icon.* Princeton University Press, 2008, p. 261.

Trillions in subsidies Black, Simon. "IMF Fossil Fuel Subsidies Data: 2023 Update." IMF Working Paper, 2023.

The IPCC says IPCC. *Global Warming of 1.5°C.* Cambridge University Press, 2022.

The power to change direction gap Sawin, Elizabeth. "This is the 'power to

change direction gap'..." Twitter, November 21, 2019.
McKibben quote Kang, Jay Caspian. "The People's Climate March: An Interview with Bill McKibben." *The New Yorker*, September 20, 2014.
Fossil fuel industry delay tactics Brulle, Robert J. "The Climate Lobby." *Climatic Change* 149 (2018), and "Institutionalizing Delay." *Climatic Change* 122 (2014).
3.5% rule Chenoweth, Erica. "The Success of Nonviolent Civil Resistance." TEDxBoulder, November 4, 2013.
Chenoweth believes it likely applies to smaller scale efforts as well Klein, Ezra. "How to Topple Dictators and Transform Society (with Erica Chenoweth)." The Ezra Klein Show, January 2, 2020.
Damon Centola's 25% research Centola, Damon. *Change: How to Make Big Things Happen*. Little, Brown Spark, 2021.
29% of people say they would act, 1% are Carman, J., et al. "Americans' Actions to Limit and Prepare For Global Warming, March 2021." Yale Program on Climate Change Communication, 2021.
Hayhoe quote Hayhoe, Katharine. "Here's How Your Climate-Related Choices Are Contagious (in a Good Way!)." TED.com, September 23, 2021.
Salt march HISTORY.com Editors. "Salt March: Definition, Date & Gandhi." HISTORY, June 10, 2010.
4.5 million INC members Tomlinson, B.R. *The Indian National Congress and the Raj, 1929-1942*. The Macmillan Press, 1976.
Suffragettes movement numbers London Museum. "Suffragettes Preparing for Women's Sunday, 21 June 1908." and Kraditor, Aileen S. *The Ideas of the Woman Suffrage Movement, 1890-1920*. Norton, 1981.
1-2 million active in civil rights movement Berg, Manfred. "National Association For The Advancement Of Colored People." In *African American Studies Center*. Oxford University Press, 2009.

CHAPTER 7

"All that you touch, you change..." Butler, Octavia E. *Parable of the Sower*. Grand Central Publishing, 2019.
Klaas quote Klaas, Brian. *Fluke: Chance, Chaos, and Why Everything We Do Matters*. Scribner, 2025.
Rohn quote Canfield, Jack, and Janet Switzer. *The Success Principles*. HarperCollins, 2005.
MIT runners study Aral, Sinan, and Christos Nicolaides. "Exercise Contagion in a Global Social Network." *Nature Communications* 8, (2017).
Happiness study Fowler, J. H, and N. A Christakis. "Dynamic Spread of Happiness in a Large Social Network." *BMJ* 337, (2008).
Christakis quote Belluck, Pam. "Strangers May Cheer You Up, Study Says." *The New York Times*, December 5, 2008.

Asch conformity experiment Asch Conformity Experiment. YouTube, 2007.
Solar panels spread through neighbors Barton-Henry, Kelsey, et al. "Decay Radius of Climate Decision for Solar Panels in the City of Fresno, USA." *Scientific Reports* 11, (2021).
How to start a movement Sivers, Derek. "How to Start a Movement." TED, 2010.
Seth Godin quote Ferriss, Tim. "How Seth Godin Manages His Life — Rules, Principles, and Obsessions." The Blog of Tim Ferriss, February 10, 2016.
Jane Goodall quote "What We Do." Jane Goodall Institute of Canada. Accessed August 29, 2025.

CHAPTER 8

Ashe quote "Black History Month 2014-2009: In His Words." Arthur Ashe Legacy. Accessed August 29, 2025.
Climate Venn diagram: The Climate Venn Diagram framework is used with the generous permission of Dr. Ayana Elizabeth Johnson and Penguin Random House LLC. All rights reserved.**'the goal is to be' quote** Johnson, Ayana Elizabeth. "How to Find Joy in Climate Action." TED, 2022.
Sawin quote Crowdsourcing Sustainability. "Systems Change, Multisolving, and the Power to Change Direction with Dr. Elizabeth Sawin." YouTube, September 9, 2021.
'Be gentle' quote Johnson, Ayana Elizabeth. "How to Find Joy in Climate Action." TED, 2022.
Drawdown's top solutions Project Drawdown. "Drawdown® Climate Solutions Library." Accessed August 29, 2025.
Drawdown's solution accelerators Project Drawdown. *The Drawdown Review: Climate Solutions for a New Decade*. 2020.
Johnson quote Johnson, Ayana Elizabeth. "How to Find Joy in Climate Action." TED, 2022.
Carbon footprints: For Burlington, VT: "Crosswalk Labs." **For Enel**: Enel Group. *2024 GHG Inventory*. 2025. **For VT**: "Greenhouse Gas Inventory | Climate Change in Vermont." Accessed August 29, 2025.
Doctorow quote Doctorow, E. L. "The Art of Fiction No. 94." *The Paris Review*, Winter 1986.

CHAPTER 9

Hayhoe quote Hayhoe, Katharine. "The Most Important Thing You Can Do to Fight Climate Change: Talk about It." TED, 2019.
34% talk about it Leiserowitz, Anthony, et al. "Climate Change in the American Mind: Beliefs & Attitudes, Spring 2024." Yale Program on Climate Change Communication. 2024.

Negligence of media Hagen, Ryan. "How the Media Continues to Fail Us on Climate & What Needs to Change." Crowdsourcing Sustainability, July 27, 2023.
Spiral of silence "Spiral of Silence - Elisabeth Noelle-Neumann."
Misperception gap study Sparkman, Gregg, Nathan Geiger, and Elke U. Weber. "Americans Experience a False Social Reality by Underestimating Popular Climate Policy Support by Nearly Half." *Nature Communications* 13, (2022).
89% Andre, Peter, et al. "Globally Representative Evidence on the Actual and Perceived Support for Climate Action." *Nature Climate Change* 14, (2024).
Yale + George Mason study "Is There a Climate 'Spiral of Silence' in America?" Yale Program on Climate Change Communication. Accessed August 30, 2025.
Deaton quote Deaton, Jeremy. "Six Charts Show Why No One Is Talking About Climate Change." *Nexus Media News*, September 29, 2016.
"Talking Climate" handbook Webster, R. & Marshall, G. *The #TalkingClimate Handbook*. Climate Outreach, 2019.
Renewables cheaper 90% of the time International Renewable Energy Agency. *Renewable Power Generation Costs in 2024*. 2025.
350k people die from US air pollution Vohra, Karn, et al. "Global Mortality from Outdoor Fine Particle Pollution Generated by Fossil Fuel Combustion." *Environmental Research* 195 (2021).
Cost of climate damages Howard, Peter, and T. Sterner. "Methodology Matters: A Careful Meta-Analysis of Climate Damages." *Environmental and Resource Economics*, 2025.
Some crops could go extinct Davis, Aaron P., et al. "High Extinction Risk for Wild Coffee Species and Implications for Coffee Sector Sustainability." *Science Advances* 5, no. 1 (2019).
Hayhoe quote Hayhoe, Katharine. "The Most Important Thing You Can Do to Fight Climate Change: Talk about It." TED, 2019.
We're wired for stories Stephens, Greg J., Lauren J. Silbert, and Uri Hasson. "Speaker-Listener Neural Coupling Underlies Successful Communication." *Proceedings of the National Academy of Sciences* 107, no. 32 (2010).
Angelou quote Widely attributed to Maya Angelou who popularized it, though its sentiment was expressed earlier by others. See full analysis at Quote Investigator.
Klein quote Klein, Ezra. "Can We Solve Global Warming Without Talking About Global Warming?" *The Washington Post*, 2010.
Saving Us by Katharine Hayhoe https://bookshop.org/p/books/saving-us-a-climate-scientist-s-case-for-hope-and-healing-in-a-divided-world-katharine-hayhoe/0603d16c63443bb3
Project Inside Out projectinsideout.net
Dear Tomorrow letter deartomorrow.org

CHAPTER 10

Kennedy quote "Florynce Kennedy." WHYY. Accessed August 31, 2025.
US is a "flawed democracy" + 71 countries have "full" or "flawed" democracy Hoey, Joan. *Democracy Index 2024*. Economist Intelligence Unit, 2025.
A republic, if you can keep it Miller, Julie. "'A Republic If You Can Keep It': Elizabeth Willing Powel, Benjamin Franklin, and the James McHenry Journal." The Library of Congress, January 6, 2022.
Walker quote "Alice Walker." Britannica, March 25, 2020.
Steffen quote Steffen, Alex. "Civitas and the Future." AlexSteffen.com, 2015.
20% vote in local elections Center for Effective Government. "The Timing of Local Elections." January 25, 2024.
No fossil fuel money pledge nofossilfuelmoney.org
Environmentalists voting stats McLendon, Russell. "Millions of Environmentalists Are Registered to Vote in the U.S. But Don't. What If They Did?" Treehugger, September 24, 2019.
70% of US elections uncontested Ballotpedia. "Analysis of Uncontested Elections, 2024." Accessed August 31, 2025.
Organizations that have made climate voting guides and scorecards Protect Our Winters: protectourwinters.org, League of Conservation Voters: lcv.org, Sunrise Movement: sunrisemovement.org, Grist: grist.org, Vote Save America: votesaveamerica.com, Climate Cabinet: climatecabinet.org, and Greenpeace: greenpeace.org.
Organizations that will help you run for office Run On Climate: https://runonclimate.org/, Run For Something: https://runforsomething.net/, Lead Locally: https://leadlocally.org/, and Climate Cabinet: https://www.climatecabinetaction.org/.

CHAPTER 11

Steffen cities quote Steffen, Alex. "Civitas and the Future." AlexSteffen.com, 2015.
Cambridge GND "Green New Deal Adopted." CambridgeGND.org. Accessed August 31, 2025.
20% vote in local elections Center for Effective Government. "The Timing of Local Elections." January 25, 2024.
Farrell quote Farrell, Jessyn. In "Community Climate Action with Seattle's Director of Sustainability." Crowdsourcing Sustainability, 2023.
Find local chapters advocacy groups 350.org and Sierra Club: https://www.sierraclub.org/chapters
Get in touch with your elected officials https://www.usa.gov/elected-officials
Climate Herald climateherald.org
Community asset mapping https://visiblenetworklabs.com/2025/04/09/

what-is-community-asset-mapping/
Climate action planning resources ICLEI: iclei.org, Run on Climate: runonclimate.org/policyresources, Greve's book, Climate Action Planning: https://bookshop.org/books/climate-action-planning-a-guide-to-creating-low-carbon-resilient-communities-revised/9781610919530. Crosswalk Labs has free local emissions data: crosswalk.io/
Power Mapping resource commonslibrary.org/power-and-power-mapping-start-here/
Citizens Assemblies Citizens' Assemblies For Ireland: Citizens' Assembly, "Previous Assemblies." For Camden: *London Borough of Camden, Camden's Citizen Assembly on the Climate Crisis.*

CHAPTER 12

Steffen quote Steffen, Alex. "Discontinuity Is the Job." *The Snap Forward*, August 9, 2021. Note: This is a similar quote. I believe the exact quote is from a lost tweet (Steffen agrees).
Alexander quote Alexander, Jamie. "Why We Haven't Stopped Climate Change -- and What to Do Now." TEDxBerlin Salon, 2024.
100 richest entities "69 of the Richest 100 Entities on the Planet Are Corporations, Not Governments." Global Justice Now, October 17, 2018.
34x more corporate lobbying Drutman, Lee. *The Business of America Is Lobbying.* Oxford University Press, 2015.
No correlation Gilens, Martin, and Benjamin I. Page. "Testing Theories of American Politics: Elites, Interest Groups, and Average Citizens." *Perspectives on Politics* 12, no. 3 (2014). For an easier read, see Represent.Us.
Largest 2000 companies have no plan "Net Zero Targets Must Become a Reality to Keep Paris Temperature Goals Live." University of Oxford, June 12, 2023.
98% of boards have no climate, biodiversity expertise "Nature Benchmark." World Benchmarking Alliance. Accessed September 1, 2025.
2x $ to candidates obstructing Bradham, Bre, Andre Tartar, and Hayley Warren. "U.S. Businesses Say One Thing on Climate Change, But Their Campaign Giving Says Another." Bloomberg, October 23, 2020.
Piper quote WorkforClimate. "Because corporations don't make decisions – people do." Instagram, March 13, 2024.
Bankrupting insurance companies Zhang, Daphne. "Storm-Driven Insurer Insolvencies Stir State Actions: Explained." Bloomberg Law, December 29, 2022. For the food sector, see: Turvey, Calum G., et al. "The Impact Of Climate Risks On U.S. Chapter 12 Farm Bankruptcies." Cornell SC Johnson College of Business Research Paper, 2025.
Carney quote Carney, Mark, François Villeroy de Galhau, and Frank Elderson.

"Open Letter on Climate-Related Financial Risks." Bank of England, April 30, 2025.
Drawdown-Aligned Business Framework https://drawdown.org/publications/climate-solutions-at-work
Bodi quote Shared directly while giving feedback on the chapter.
10x more $ spent against climate action Brulle, Robert J. "The Climate Lobby: a Sectoral Analysis of Lobbying Spending on Climate Change in the USA, 2000 to 2016." *Climatic Change* 149, (2018).
Climate Voice climatevoice.org/about
Microsoft AI for fossil fuels "Oil in the Cloud." Greenpeace, May 19, 2020.
20%-30% of $ in banks Alexander, Jamie Beck, Paul Moinester, and Julian Kraus-Polk. *Saving for the Planet*. Project Drawdown and Topo Finance, 2023.
Google $ emissions Vaccaro, James, and Paul Moinester. *The Carbon Bankroll Report*. Climate Safe Lending Network et al., 2022.
Greening Cash Action Guide https://exponentialroadmap.org/wp-content/uploads/2023/08/Greening-Cash-Action-Guide.pdf
Carbon collective: carboncollective.co/401k, **Sphere:** oursphere.org, **Premiums for the Planet**: premiumsfortheplanet.com
Examples of corporate action For The Guardian: "Guardian to Ban Advertising from Fossil Fuel Firms." For Netflix: "Telling Climate Stories at Scale." For Ørsted: "The Top 20 Business Transformations of the Last Decade."
83% of employees want to work on climate *Every Job Is a Climate Job*. Kite Insights, 2022.
"Get Ready, Get Set, Get Organised" playbook https://www.workforclimate.org/resources-playbooks/influence-playbooks
"Starting a Circle at Work" guide https://www.allwecansave.earth/starting-a-circle-at-work
Alexander quote Alexander, Jamie Beck. In "Every Job Is a Climate Job." Crowdsourcing Sustainability, January 7, 2022.
Frischmann quote From a conversation with Frischmann, August 2025. A similar quote can be found here.
59% C-suite leaders "Engaged Employees Are Asking Their Leaders to Take Climate Action." Deloitte Insights, November 9, 2023.
Sustainability teams less than 1% Wilkinson, Drew. In "Every Job Is a Climate Job." Work on Climate, 2025.
Employee surveys can lead to big wins Kratzmann, Emily. "Meet the Engineer Who Switched His Firm to Renewable Energy." WorkforClimate, May 20, 2025.
Power mapping chart "Climate Solutions at Work." Project Drawdown, March 2025.
Joint letters For Amazon: "Public Letter to Jeff Bezos and the Amazon Board of Directors." For Immediate Media: "Letter to Tom - Asking Our CEO for

Organisational Leadership on the Climate Crisis."
Climate solutions at work "Climate Solutions at Work." Project Drawdown, March 2025.
WorkforClimate Playbooks "Climate Leadership for Employees": https://www.workforclimate.org/access-playbook/access-our-climate-leadership-playbook, "Emissions": https://www.workforclimate.org/resources/emissions, "Energy": https://www.workforclimate.org/resources/energy, "Money": https://www.workforclimate.org/resources/money
WorkforClimate 3-month course www.workforclimate.org/academy
Work on Climate slack workonclimate.org
Drawdown's Job Function Action Guides "Job Function Action Guides." Project Drawdown, August 27, 2024.
Apple incentivizes executives *Apple 14A Proxy Statement*. Apple, 2021.
General Mills "Climate Action @ Work." Project Drawdown, 2024.
Rodriguez quote Bodi, Aiyana. "Answering an Existential Call for Climate Action." Project Drawdown, August 20, 2024.
Wilkinson quote Smith, Sarah. "Drew Wilkinson Turned 10,000 Microsoft Employees on to Climate Action." WorkforClimate, July 23, 2024.
Microsoft $1 billion fund Smith, Brad. "Microsoft Will Be Carbon Negative by 2030." The Official Microsoft Blog, January 16, 2020.

CHAPTER 13

Winston quote Winston, Andrew. In "16 Sustainability Leaders Weigh In: How YOU Can Help To Reverse Global Warming." Crowdsourcing Sustainability, January 2019.
Wind and solar job growth "Fastest Growing Occupations." Bureau of Labor Statistics. Accessed September 2, 2025.
Daniel Hill advice From an email exchange, July 2025.
Excellent climate courses Regenerative Intelligence: regenintel.earth/regenintel-fellowship, Terra.do: Terra.do, Climatebase: climatebase.org/fellowship
Climate communities on slack Work on Climate, WorkforClimate, and My Climate Journey.
Climate groups by profession/industry https://crowdsourcingsustainability.org/climate-groups-by-profession-industry/
OpenDoorClimate https://www.opendoorclimate.com/directory
Climate Job Boards Green Jobs Board browngirlgreen.com/greenjobs, Climatebase climatebase.org, The Bloom readtobloom.com, Ed's Clean Energy & Sustainability Jobs List edscleanenergysustainabilityjobs.com, Queer Outdoor & Environmental Job Board queeroutdoors.net/job-board, Green Job Search greenjobs.greenjobsearch.org, Nature Tech Jobs naturetech.io, Terra.do terra.do/climate-jobs/

Shortage of green jobs in future "Green Jobs Grow Twice as Fast as Workers with Green Skills." World Economic Forum, February 2024.

CHAPTER 14

Mandela quote Mandela, Nelson. "Address at the Launch of the Nelson Mandela Children's Fund." Pretoria, May 8, 1995.

Thunberg Kottasova, Ivana, and Eliza Mackintosh. "Teen Activist Blames Davos Elite for Climate Crisis." CNN, January 25, 2019.

Many schools are not safe and healthy, especially in BIPOC, low-income communities Williams, Elinor, and Akira Drake Rodriguez. *Funding a Green New Deal for Public Schools*. Climate and Community Project, 2023.

Health, attendance, and grades improve Williams, Elinor, and Akira Drake Rodriguez. *Funding a Green New Deal for Public Schools*. Climate and Community Project, 2023.

Improves mental health M., Clayton, S., & Hill, A. N. *Mental Health and Our Changing Climate: Impacts, Inequities, Responses*. American Psychological Association and ecoAmerica, 2021.

Batesville Schools story Ellfeldt, Avery. "This School Turned Solar Savings into Better Teacher Pay." Canary Media, October 16, 2020.

Romm I first used this quote in 2018, but can't locate it now. Romm believes it is from a speech. Closest version is in his book: Romm, Joseph J. *Climate Change: What Everyone Needs to Know*. Joseph Romm, 2022.

Demand for sustainability skills 2x higher than supply by 2050 *Global Climate Talent Stocktake*. LinkedIn, 2024.

Nakagawa Darley, James. "LinkedIn's Global Talent Stocktake: Green Skills in Demand." *Sustainability Magazine*, October 2, 2024.

healthcare sector = 8.5% of emissions Eckelman, Matthew J., et al. "Health Care Pollution And Public Health Damage In The United States: An Update." *Health Affairs* 39, no. 12 (2020).

86% and 42% K-12 teachers Kamenetz, Anya. "Most Teachers Don't Teach Climate Change; 4 In 5 Parents Wish They Did." NPR, April 22, 2019.

Subject to climate subjecttoclimate.org/

NJ climate curriculum Solomon, Randall. "Educators Integrate Climate Change Instruction into the Classroom." New Jersey Education Association, September 29, 2022.

Leading universities stats "Participants & Reports | Institutions | STARS Reports." Accessed September 3, 2025.

Lenier Stahl, Jess. "Grist 50 2024." Grist, September 5, 2024.

Climate Emotions Toolkit for Educators https://www.neefusa.org/what-we-do/health/climate-emotions-toolkit

Sample resolutions New Buildings Institute: https://newbuildings.org/resource/

interactive-map-of-carbon-neutral-school-districts/
Green New Deal for Schools Campaign Guidebook https://drive.google.com/file/d/1O-kgmUrTjwM1MM3DznGzZBrAzszinqXh/view?usp=sharing
K-12 Climate Action Plan https://www.thisisplaneted.org/img/K12-ClimateActionPlan-Complete-Screen.pdf
How to Pass a School District-Wide Climate Policy Toolkit https://www.dpsclimateaction.org/toolkit
Denver schools stats "Sustainability | Denver Public Schools." Accessed September 3, 2025.
School Board Member Action Toolkit https://www.undauntedk12.org/for-school-boards
Rewiring America https://www.rewiringamerica.org/go-electric/electric-schools
STARS stars.aashe.org
Green New Deal for Campus Campaign Guidebook https://docs.google.com/document/d/1BDuy7pDzMX2UnrcnYFLfLl10y_4p5Vm9/edit?tab=t.0#heading=h.2ojxkw1ks8db
Higher Ed Climate Action Plan https://www.thisisplaneted.org/img/HigherEdClimateActionPlan.pdf
Rajbhandari Preston, Caroline. "How Can Schools Keep Kids Safe in a Warming World?" *The Hechinger Report*, September 16, 2024. (Plus information from emails with Shiva Rajbhandari).

CHAPTER 15

Thunberg quote Thunberg, Greta. "'Our House Is on Fire': Greta Thunberg, 16, Urges Leaders to Act on Climate." The Guardian, January 25, 2019.
Per capita footprints European Commission, Joint Research Centre, and IEA. GHG Emissions of All World Countries. 2024.
Statue of liberty analogy An original analogy based on data from the National Park Service and the University of Michigan's "Carbon Footprint Factsheet."
$140k "Emissions Inequality Dashboard." Accessed September 4, 2025.
1%'s emissions equal bottom 66% + visual Khalfan, Ashfaq, et al. Climate Equality: A Planet for the 99%. Oxfam International, 2023.
Earth Hero calculator earthhero.org
Chart of average US footprint "CoolClimate Calculator." UC Berkeley. Accessed September 4, 2025. (Note: I share multiple "consumption-based" footprint calculations in this chapter, which vary slightly but are all in the ~18-19 tonne range.)
Round trip flight 1.5 tonnes "CO_2 Emissions Calculator." myclimate. Accessed September 4, 2025.
9 sq m of ice melt per ton of CO_2 Notz, Dirk, and Julienne Stroeve. "Observed

Arctic Sea-Ice Loss Directly Follows Anthropogenic CO_2 Emission." Science 354, no. 6313 (2016).

Rewiring America's guides "Electrify Everything in Your Home" and guide for renters "Personal Electrification Planner."

US food waste "Food Waste FAQs." USDA. Accessed September 3, 2025.

GHGs for food chart Hannah Ritchie, Pablo Rosado, and Max Roser (2022) – "Environmental Impacts of Food Production" Published online at OurWorldinData.org. https://ourworldindata.org/environmental-impacts-of-food

Replace beef with chicken Willits-Smith, Amelia, et al. "Addressing the Carbon Footprint, Healthfulness, and Costs of Self-Selected Diets in the USA." The Lancet Planetary Health 4, no. 3 (2020).

Vegetarian and vegan diets Maslin, Mark. "Climatarian, Flexitarian, Vegetarian, Vegan: Which Diet Is Best for the Planet?" TED.com, September 7, 2022.

20% to 37% Williamson, Katie, et al. Climate Change Needs Behavior Change. Rare, 2018.

CHAPTER 16

"Follow the money" Pakula, Alan J., dir. All The President's Men. Warner Bros., 1976.

$7.9 trillion Rainforest Action Network, BankTrack, Indigenous Environmental Network, Oil Change International, Reclaim Finance, Sierra Club, Urgewald, and CEED. Banking on Climate Chaos 2025. 2025.

7% in fossil fuels "Search Funds | Fossil Free Funds." Accessed September 9, 2025.

US Retirement accounts Montes, Andrew. "Our Retirement Savings Own One Fifth of U.S. Fossil Fuel Stocks." Fossil Free Funds, February 1, 2024.

No new fossil fuel development International Energy Agency. Net Zero by 2050. 2021.

Guterres quote Harvey, Fiona. "Fossil Fuel Firms 'Have Humanity by the Throat', Says UN Head in Blistering Attack." The Guardian, June 17, 2022.

19% lent to carbon intensive projects + 0.24 tonnes/$1k Alexander, Jamie Beck, Paul Moinester, and Julian Kraus-Polk. Saving for the Planet. Project Drawdown and Topo Finance, 2023.

$8k and $62k Board of Governors of the Federal Reserve System. "Changes in U.S. Family Finances from 2019 to 2022." Federal Reserve Bulletin, October 18, 2023.

Bank.Green: https://bank.green/, **Bank for Good EU**: https://bankforgoodeu.com/

Third Act's "How to Switch to Better Banks & Credit Cards FAQs" https://thirdact.org/resources/how-to-switch-to-better-banks-credit-cards-faqs/

Bank.Green's list of sustainable banks https://bank.green/sustainable-eco-banks
Investing in market footprint "iShares Core S&P 500 ETF | Carbon Footprint." Fossil Free Funds. Accessed September 5, 2025.
$87k and $334k Board of Governors of the Federal Reserve System. "Changes in U.S. Family Finances from 2019 to 2022." Federal Reserve Bulletin, October 18, 2023.
Most people want to invest sustainably "Sustainable Signals." Morgan Stanley, October 27, 2021.
Risky to invest in fossil fuels "Financial Risks of Unsustainable Investments." Invest Your Values. Accessed September 5, 2025.
Regulinski paraphrase Regulinski, James. In "Sustainable Investing Builds the Future We Want." Crowdsourcing Sustainability, 2023.
Fossil Free Funds fossilfreefunds.org
Fund managers fossil fuel %'s "Fund Families." Fossil Free Funds. Accessed September 5, 2025.
Morgan Stanley report Sustainable Reality. Morgan Stanley, 2019.
ESG greenwashing study As You Sow. "Lack of Truth in Labeling in ESG Mutual Funds and ETFs." January 11, 2022.
Carbon Collective https://www.carboncollective.co/ **ETHO ETF:** https://ethocapital.com/performance-ecli-us
As You Sow auto-voting https://www.asyousow.org/reports/proxy-voting-guidelines-2025
Climate and FF investments 2024 Climate Policy Initiative. Global Landscape of Climate Finance 2025. 2025.
$40 trillion "Homepage - Global Fossil Fuel Commitments Database." Accessed August 28, 2025.

CHAPTER 17

Washington quote Washington, Booker T. *Up from Slavery*. Cosimo, Inc., 2007.
1.5% of charitable donations Esmaeili, Narine, et al. *Funding Trends 2024*. Climateworks, 2024.
Netflix revenue Netflix, Inc. *10-K Report*. 2025.
Sunrise Movement sunrisemovement.org
350.org 350.org
Climate Changemakers climatechangemakers.org
Extinction Rebellion rebellion.global
The All We Can Save Project allwecansave.earth
Third Act thirdact.org
Climate Emergency Fund climateemergencyfund.org
Global Greengrants Fund greengrants.org
WE ACT for Environmental Justice weact.org

Taproot Earth taprootearth.org
Rainforest Foundation US rainforestfoundation.org
Indigenous Environmental Network ienearth.org
Honor the Earth honorearth.org
The Deep South Center for Environmental Justice dscej.org
Intersectional Environmentalist intersectionalenvironmentalist.com
Environmental Voter Project environmentalvoter.org
Run On Climate runonclimate.org
Global Solutions Alliance gsa.earth/
Multisolving Institute multisolving.org
Climate Curve keelingcurveprize.org
Rewiring America rewiringamerica.org
Evergreen Action evergreenaction.com/
Grist grist.org
Inside Climate News insideclimatenews.org
ClimateVoice climatevoice.org
WorkforClimate workforclimate.org
CAMFED camfed.org
ClientEarth clientearth.org
Earthjustice earthjustice.org
67% give to charity Childress, Rasheeda. "Charitable Donations Continue to Decline, down 2.1% in 2023, According to a New Giving USA Report." AP News, June 25, 2024.
2% of income to charity Brown, Helen. "Factoring in Compensation." Helen Brown Group, August 17, 2023.
Median income "Median Personal Income in the United States." FRED, St. Louis Fed, September 10, 2024.

CHAPTER 18

Douglass quote Douglass, Frederick. "West India Emancipation." Speech, Canandaigua, NY, 1857.
XR shut down London + UK declares climate emergency Blackall, Molly. "Extinction Rebellion Protests Block Traffic in Five UK Cities." *The Guardian*, July 15, 2019.
UK net zero law "UK Becomes First Major Economy to Pass Net Zero Emissions Law." GOV.UK, June 27, 2019.
Civil resistance definition Chenoweth, Erica. *Civil Resistance: What Everyone Needs to Know*. Oxford University Press, 2021.
3.5% rule Chenoweth, Erica. "The Success of Nonviolent Civil Resistance." TEDxBoulder, November 4, 2013.
Pillars of support visual made by me, inspired by The Commons Library's

"Pillars of Power."
Chenoweth quote Chenoweth, Erica. *Civil Resistance*, p. 32.
Abujbara quote Abujbara, Juman. In *Beautiful Rising: Creative Resistance from the Global South*. Between the Lines, 2018.
Birmingham campaign Engler, Mark, and Paul Engler. *This Is an Uprising: How Nonviolent Revolt Is Shaping the Twenty-First Century*. Bold Type Books, 2017.
Piven quote Piven, Frances Fox. *Challenging Authority: How Ordinary People Change America*. Rowman & Littlefield, 2006.
Ancient Egypt, Haudenosaunee Clan Mothers Chenoweth, Erica. *Civil Resistance*, p. 7.
Salt march HISTORY.com Editors. "Salt March: Definition, Date & Gandhi." HISTORY, June 10, 2010.
Rosa parks "Montgomery Bus Boycott." The Martin Luther King, Jr. Research and Education Institute.
Anti apartheid movement "The Anti-Apartheid Struggle in South Africa (1912-1992)." ICNC.
Chenoweth quote Chenoweth, Erica. *Civil Resistance*, p. 27.
Sunrise popularized GND Lawrence, William, et al. "From the Green New Deal to the Inflation Reduction Act." *Convergence Magazine*, October 24, 2023.
More than 7.5 million people "7.6 Million People Demand Action after Week of Climate Strikes." 350.org, September 27, 2019.
Scotland, NZ, European Commission net zero laws For Scotland: "Climate Change Bill." For New Zealand: "Climate Change Response (Zero Carbon) Amendment Act 2019." For the European Commission: "The European Green Deal."
Keystone XL Adler, Ben. "The inside Story of the Campaign That Killed Keystone XL." Vox, November 7, 2015.
Keys to successful campaign Chenoweth, Erica, and Maria J. Stephan. *Why Civil Resistance Works: The Strategic Logic of Nonviolent Conflict*. Columbia University Press, 2011.
198 Methods of Nonviolent Action https://www.brandeis.edu/peace-conflict/pdfs/198-methods-non-violent-action.pdf
Additional research Engler, Mark, and Paul Engler. *This Is an Uprising*.
Lewis quote Bote, Joshua. "'Get in Good Trouble, Necessary Trouble': Rep. John Lewis in His Own Words." *USA TODAY*.

CHAPTER 19

Klein quote Klein, Naomi. "Capitalism Is Waging a War on the Earth." Speech at the Festival of Dangerous Ideas, Sydney Opera House, September 5, 2015.
Tens of millions Internal Displacement Monitoring Centre. *2025 Global Report on Internal Displacement*. 2025.

Possibly 1.2 billion displaced by 2050 Institute for Economics & Peace. *Ecological Threat Register 2020.* September 2020.

CHAPTER 20

Hạnh quote Hạnh, Nhất, and Sister True Dedication. *Zen and the Art of Saving the Planet.* HarperOne, 2021.
Meadows quote Meadows, Donella. "Leverage Points: Places to Intervene in a System." The Academy for Systems Change.
Harari quote Harari, Yuval Noah. "Why Humans Run the World." TED, July 24, 2015.
Humanity's superpower Harari, Yuval N. *Sapiens: A Brief History of Humankind.* Harper, 2015.
Sawin quote Sawin, Elizabeth. "The Beauty of Multisolving." Entangled World, October 10, 2024.
Atoms transform "Law of Conservation of Mass." Chemistry LibreTexts, June 22, 2016.
Businessman with kids cartoon Toro, Tom. "Yes, the planet got destroyed..." Cartoon. *The New Yorker*, November 26, 2012.
Obomsawin quote Obomsawin, Alanis. In *Who is the Chairman of this Meeting?*, edited by Ralph Osborne, 1972.
Mitchell quote Mitchell, Sherri. *Sacred Instructions: Indigenous Wisdom for Living Spirit-Based Change.* North Atlantic Books, 2018.
Boggs quote Boggs, Grace Lee. "Reimagine Everything." March 2, 2012.

CHAPTER 21

Billions want to do more American Psychological Association. "Majority of US Adults Believe Climate Change Is Most Important Issue Today." 2020.
Steffen quote Steffen, Alex. "The climate emergency is not an issue, it's an era. It's when we live." Twitter, September 20, 2019.
Heumann quote Heumann, Judith E., and Kristen Joiner. *Being Heumann: An Unrepentant Memoir of a Disability Rights Activist.* Beacon Press, 2020.
Sawin quote Crowdsourcing Sustainability. "Systems Change, Multisolving, and the Power to Change Direction with Dr. Elizabeth Sawin." YouTube, September 9, 2021.
That's what we'll all judge ourselves by on our deathbeds The "deathbed test" is a powerful exercise. I first journaled on it in 2016, inspired by Buddhism, Stoicism, and Tara Brach - it changed my life. I also want to thank Sister True Dedication, who explores these ideas beautifully in Thich Nhất Hạnh's Zen and the Art of Saving the Planet (HarperOne, 2021).

About the Author

I'm a big sustainability nerd on a mission to help build a safe, healthy, and just world. This has led to things I never would have expected: writing a climate newsletter with 200,000+ subscribers from 150+ countries, starting the nonprofit Crowdsourcing Sustainability, speaking at dozens of events, and empowering thousands of people to make the places they live and work more sustainable. My work has been recognized by the UN, TEDx, and LinkedIn.

When I'm not nerding out on climate action, I'm usually with family and friends, taking a walk in the woods, learning, playing soccer, watching sunsets, or seeing how many first sips I can get out of a coffee oreo milkshake.

I hope you found this book helpful. If you want to stay in touch, sign up for my newsletter, "Act on Climate" – I'd love to hear from you!

www.ingramcontent.com/pod-product-compliance
Lightning Source LLC
Chambersburg PA
CBHW020539030426
42337CB00013B/909